ARBITRAGE

Arbitrage
Elements of Financial Economics

Michael Allingham
Professor of Economic Theory
University of Kent

St. Martin's Press   New York

First published in the United States of America in 1991

Printed in Great Britain

ISBN 0–312–06202–8

Library of Congress Cataloging-in-Publication Data
Allingham, Michael.
Arbitrage: elements of financial economics / Michael Allingham.
p.   cm.
Includes bibliographical references (p.   ) and index.
ISBN 0–312–06202–8
1. Arbitrage.   2. Securities—Valuation.   I. Title.
HG4521.A45   1991
332.64'5—dc20   91–14581
                                                          CIP

Contents

v

Preface

This book uses the concept of arbitrage to value securities, that is, to construct the elements of financial economics.

The importance of arbitrage in the context of certainty has long been recognised: it is, for example discussed in detail in Walras's *Elements of Pure Economics* of 1874. But its use in the absence of certainty, and thus in financial economics, is a more recent development, originating (at least explicitly) in the work of Black and Scholes on options in 1973. In this context it provides an alternative to the concept of equilibrium which has provided the central paradigm of financial economics since the development of the capital asset pricing model by Sharpe and Lintner in 1964 and 1965.

The book is divided into three parts. Part I develops the foundations for the study: it introduces the concepts of securities and arbitrage (Chapter 1) and establishes the basic arbitrage theorem, that security prices may be expressed as expected discounted values (Chapter 2). Part II applies the basic theorem in a single-period setting: it develops a version of the capital asset pricing model under exact arbitrage (Chapter 3) and the arbitrage pricing technique under approximate arbitrage (Chapter 4). Part III extends the discussion to a many-period setting: it uses static arbitrage to value futures and related securities (Chapter 5), dynamic arbitrage to value options and other derivatives (Chapter 6), and, as a coda, information arbitrage to investigate market efficiency (Chapter 7).

Within each chapter the basic theory is developed quite comprehensively, while empirical evidence and applications are discussed more selectively. The presentation assumes an understanding of only the most basic concepts of mathematics and statistics, detailed references being provided in the few instances where more advanced concepts are introduced. An appendix to the chapter discusses any connection with the equilibrium approach to the subject, while works drawn on, and related works, are listed in the chapter's bibliography.

MICHAEL ALLINGHAM

Part I
Foundations

1 Securities and Arbitrage

This book uses the concept of arbitrage to value securities. This introductory chapter provides an informal introduction to securities, arbitrage and related concepts.

FINANCIAL ECONOMICS

Economics is concerned with commodities, money and securities. Commodities are best described by example: goods such as wheat and gold, services such as labour and freight, and assets such as land and machines are all commodities. Money, such as dollars or sterling, is not a commodity but a means of exchange of commodities. And securities, such as bonds and stocks, are neither commodities nor money but contracts for the exchange of commodities or money.

Real economics explains the relative prices of commodities, such as the price of wheat in terms of gold. Monetary economics proceeds to explain the value of (an intrinsically worthless) money, and thus the absolute, or money, prices of commodities. Financial economics, taking the values of commodities and money as established, is concerned with the prices of securities.

A fundamental difference between real and monetary economics on the one hand and financial economics on the other is that the former is only secondarily concerned with uncertainty: its primary purpose is the explanation of prices under certainty. But uncertainty is central to the latter: given the prices of commodities and money the pricing of securities under certainty is trivial.

A further basic difference between real and monetary economics and financial economics lies in their central paradigms. The central paradigm of the former is the

3

concept of equilibrium prices, that is, prices at which all planned purchases and sales are consistent. The central paradigm of the latter, however, is the concept of arbitrage-free prices, that is, prices at which there are no profit opportunities which involve no outlay or risk.

While the equilibrium paradigm may also be applied to the pricing of securities it is less powerful than the arbitrage paradigm in this context. The explanation of equilibrium prices of securities requires the enumeration of both the universe of securities and the universe of holders of securities, that is, of agents. The explanation of arbitrage-free prices, however, requires the enumeration only of the particular securities under consideration. Since the universes of potential securities and of agents are not observable this difference is of practical as well as theoretical importance.

DATES AND STATES

Securities are contracts for the transfer of money or commodities on various dates and on the occurrence of various states of the world.

Dates are to be understood in their usual sense, commencing with the present. Only a finite number of dates is considered. This implies that the horizon must be bounded, though may be arbitrarily large, say a billion years. It also implies that time must unfold in discrete intervals, though these may be arbitrarily small, say milliseconds.

The case where there are only two dates, say today and tomorrow, is of particular interest. In this case a state is a complete description of the world tomorrow: the weather, peoples' tastes, technical opportunities and so forth. For example, the states may be 'sun', 'rain', 'both sun and rain' and 'neither sun nor rain'. States are defined so that precisely one must occur. As with dates, and with analogous implications, only a finite number of states is considered.

In the case where there are many dates (say Monday, Tuesday and so forth) a state is a complete description of the world on each of these dates. For example, the states may now be 'sun Monday sun Tuesday', 'sun Monday rain Tuesday', 'rain Monday sun Tuesday' and so forth. As time unfolds some states become redundant. For example, if there is no sun on Monday then states such as 'sun Monday sun Tuesday' are irrelevant on Tuesday.

The evolution of states over time may be represented by the tree, or nodal, structure of states, as illustrated in Figure 1.1. In this structure a node represents a date (for example, Monday) and a set of possible states on that date (for example, 'sun Monday sun Tuesday' and 'sun Monday rain Tuesday'). A state is represented by a path from the single node now to one of the nodes on the last date (for example, 'sun Monday sun Tuesday').

Potential parties to security contracts are known as agents. It is assumed that on each date all agents agree which states are possible, that is, they have the same information about the past. However, they will typically have different views of the future, that is, they will typically assign different probabilities to the various possible states.

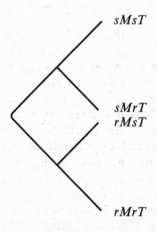

Figure 1.1

SECURITIES

More precisely, a security is a transferable contract between two parties (a short and a long) which specifies, for each date (in the future) and state, the (positive or negative) amounts of some specified money or commodity which the short is to transfer to the long. For example, a contract specifying that the short transfer $1 to the long (or equivalently that the long transfer −$1 to the short) tomorrow if there is sun, while no transfers are to be made if there is not, is a security.

By extension, a contract for the transfer of securities, as well as of money or commodities, on various dates and states is also to be considered a security. This is because such a contract indirectly specifies the transfers of money or commodities to be made on each date and state. Securities which specify transfers of money or commodities directly are primary securities, while those which do so only indirectly, through specifying transfers of securities, are derivative securities.

This extension involves no circularity, that is we do not have to consider *a* being a contract for the transfer of *b* and *b* being a contract for the transfer of *a*. This is because transfers are to be made on dates in the future, so that *b* would have to be dated after *a* and *a* dated after *b*, which is impossible. Nor do we have to consider *a* being a contract for the transfer of *b*, *b* being a contract for the transfer of *c*, and so forth indefinitely. This is because *b* would have to be dated after *a*, *c* dated after *b*, and so forth indefinitely, which is impossible with a finite number of dates.

Quantities of securities are measured in some given units. If one contract differs from another only in that the transfers specified by the first on each date and state are a constant (positive or negative) multiple of those specified by the second then the two contracts are considered to consist of different quantities of the same security. For example, if a contract *a* specifies the transfer from the short to the long of $1 in all states tomorrow, *b* specifies the transfer of $2 similarly, and *c* specifies the transfer of −$1 similarly then *b* may be considered to consist of two units of *a* and *c* may be considered to consist of minus one unit of a. Alternatively, a may be considered to consist of half a unit of b and c may be considered to consist of minus half a unit of b, and so forth.

A simple example of a security is a (default-free) bond. This is a claim to interest and redemption payments on various dates, the payments being the same in all states.

A more complex example of a security is an equity, or share in a company. This is a claim to dividend payments on various dates. However, different payments are made in different states: a large payment may be made in the state 'expansion' and a small payment in the state 'contraction'.

Forwards and options are also securities. A gold forward involves at its maturity the delivery of a commodity, gold, by one party and the payment of money, the contract price, by the other; each transfer is the same in all states (though typically the value of the gold delivered will not be). A (European call) gold option effectively involves the same transfers in all states in which the value of gold at its maturity exceeds the contract price, and no transfers in all other states. Bond forwards and options are also securities, though as bonds are themselves securities these are derivative rather than primary securities.

However, money is not a security as it is not a contract (though a transferable loan of money, that is, a bond, is). And for the same reason, commodities are not securities (though shares in companies which own commodities, and commodity futures and options, are).

One reason for distinguishing between securities on the one hand and money or commodities to which these may be closely related on the other, say between gold futures and gold, is that the holding of money or commodities may in itself confer some benefits or costs: gold may be ornamental, but may need to be insured. But the holding of securities in itself confers no benefits or costs: a gold future is simply a contract.

A further reason for distinguishing between securities and money or commodities is that an agent's holdings of securities may be negative. However, because of their physical nature, holdings of money or commodities cannot be negative: agents may borrow money (or commodities), but this constitutes issuing bonds, which are securities, rather than holding negative amounts of money.

A security is created by a contract being made between a short and a long. If when this occurs the quantity of the security held by the long is one unit, say, then the quantity held by the short must be minus one unit. This implies that the market holding of a security, that is the sum of all agents' holdings, is always zero. For example, the market holding of a bond is the sum of the positive holdings of the longs (mainly investors) and the counterbalancing negative holdings of the shorts (mainly the issuer). This property again distinguishes securities from money or commodities, the market holdings of which, being the sum of all individuals' holdings, typically are positive.

If, for some security, some agents are excluded from consideration then the total holdings of the remaining agents will typically be non-zero. For example, if, for government bonds, governments are excluded then total private holdings will be positive; and if, for equities, companies are excluded then total individual holdings will be positive. However, the exclusion of certain agents, or equivalently the definition of total holdings of securities, is arbitrary.

A satisfactory theory of security prices should not involve the specification of arbitrary total holdings, or equivalently of arbitrarily excluded agents. Indeed, since the universe of agents is unobservable such a theory should not involve the enumeration of these agents. Further, since the universe of securities is also unobservable a satisfactory theory of security prices should not involve any enumeration of this universe.

THE SECURITIES MARKET

The environment in which securities are created and transferred between agents is the securities market. Two assumptions are made on the nature of this market.

The first assumption is that the market is frictionless, in that there are no transactions costs, taxes, or other restrictions on trade. This simplification is justified, at least for many securities, by the presence of certain agents, such as institutions, which have very low transactions costs and no other restrictions on trade, and by that fact collectively tend to dominate the market.

The second assumption is that the market is competitive in that any quantities of securities, positive or negative, large or small (including fractional), may be traded at the prices ruling in the market. This assumption is justified, again for many securities, by the existence of a large number of agents none of which individually dominates the market.

These two assumptions of frictionless and competitive markets may alternatively be interpreted as a restriction on the securities under consideration. This is to say that attention is restricted to securities which are traded in frictionless competitive markets.

An indication of the importance of securities markets is provided by the total open interest, that is, the total value of all long (or equivalently of all short) holdings of securities. A breakdown of the (short side of the) open interest of the two main classes of securities in the three main geographical regions at the beginning of 1990, all expressed as percentages of the respective annual incomes, is given in Table 1.1 (International Stock Exchange, 1990).

Table 1.1

	Bonds	*Equities*	*Total*
Europe	73	79	152
North America	28	73	101
Pacific	64	259	323
Total	48	108	156

It is apparent that securities are of major importance in the world economy.

PRICES AND ARBITRAGE

It is assumed that money and commodities are also traded in frictionless competitive markets and always have positive value. One form of money (or one commodity), designated dollars, is adopted as a standard unit of value.

A security may be considered to be a contract for the receipt of (positive or negative amounts of) dollars on various dates and states. For example, a forward contract specifying the delivery of an ounce of gold and the receipt of $500 tomorrow in all states may be considered to be a contract to receive $1 tomorrow in all states in which the price of an ounce of gold tomorrow is $499, to receive −$1 tomorrow in all states where this price is $501, and so forth.

A class of securities which is of particular interest is that of limited liability securities. A limited liability security is a security which specifies negative receipts on no dates or states and positive receipts on some. Since all money and commodities have positive value the definition of a limited liability security is independent of the particular unit of value adopted.

A class of limited liability securities of particular interest is that of risk-free securities. A risk-free security is a security which, on each date, specifies the same receipt (negative on no date and positive on some) in each state. However, the definition of a risk-free security does depend on the particular unit of value adopted. For example, if the sterling–dollar exchange rate differs in different states then the receipt of $1 in each state implies the receipt of different amounts of sterling in different states.

The price of a security on some date is the amount of dollars for which a unit of the security may be exchanged, that is, bought or sold, on that date. This price need not be pos-itive: indeed, whether it is positive or negative depends on the arbitrary definition of a unit of the security. However, as will be seen, the prices of limited liability securities are positive.

Since the choice of the standard unit of value is arbitrary a satisfactory theory of security prices should not depend on this choice. That is, the dollar price of a security whose payments and receipts are designated in dollars should be the same as the sterling price of the same security when the payments and receipts are designated in sterling.

A portfolio is a list of holdings of securities (one for each security). For example, a portfolio may consist of half a bond, minus two stocks and zero futures (that is, long half a unit of bonds, short two units of stock and neutral in futures). Since portfolios are collections of contracts each for the receipt of dollars on various dates and states they have the same properties as securities. Thus limited liability and risk-free portfolios are analogous to limited liability and risk-free securities respectively: a limited liability portfolio is a portfolio involving negative receipts on no dates or states and positive receipts on some, while a risk-free portfolio is one involving, on each date, the same (negative on no date and positive on some) receipt in each state.

Given a list of security prices (one for each security) the cost of a portfolio is the sum of the costs, at these prices, of its constituents. For example, if the prices of bonds and stocks are both $10 then the cost of the portfolio specified in the example above is $-$15; the fact that this is negative indicates that the acquisition of the portfolio involves a receipt today rather than a payment.

Given a list of prices an arbitrage portfolio is a costless limited liability portfolio. More precisely, it is a portfolio whose cost at these prices is zero or negative and which involves negative receipts in no states and positive receipts in some.

Consider an example with three securities and two states. The dollar receipts specified by the various securities in each state are given in Table 1.2. If the price of a unit of each security is $1 then a portfolio consisting of two units of a, minus one of b and minus one of c (that is long two a and short one b and one c) is an arbitrage portfolio: its cost is zero and it produces $3 in each state.

The existence of an arbitrage portfolio implies that all agents have the possibility of acquiring dollars with no outlay or risk, that is, of a 'free lunch'. Indeed, since doubling an arbitrage portfolio doubles the receipts produced by it but

Table 1.2

Security	Sun	Rain
a	2	2
b	1	0
c	0	1

leaves it costless the existence of an arbitrage portfolio implies that all agents have the possibility of acquiring unlimited amounts of dollars with no outlay or risk, that is, of a 'money pump'. The basic premise of arbitrage theory is that there are no arbitrage portfolios. Since the existence of an arbitrage portfolio depends on the prices of the securities this premise is equivalent to the premise that security prices are arbitrage-free prices, that is, prices at which there are no arbitrage portfolios.

An immediate implication of this premise is that the price of a limited liability security (or portfolio) is positive. If it were not then a portfolio consisting of one unit of the security would be costless and thus, being a limited liability portfolio, an arbitrage portfolio.

In the above example a portfolio which is long in a and short in b and c equally is always an arbitrage portfolio if the price of a is less than the sum of the prices of b and c. And the negative of such a portfolio is always an arbitrage portfolio if the price of a is greater than the sum of the prices of b and c. It follows that in the absence of arbitrage the price of a must be equal to sum of the prices of b and c.

However, apart from requiring that all three prices are positive, because all securities have limited liability, arbitrage makes no further restrictions on prices. In particular, it makes no restriction on the relative prices of b and c.

The restrictions on prices made by arbitrage theory are independent of the unit of value, the universe of agents and the probabilities which agents assign to states, and the universe of securities. Although the unit of value is mentioned in the example the argument employed may be repeated with the same conclusion whatever unit is employed. The universe of agents and the probabilities which agents assign to states are not mentioned, and therefore irrelevant. And the universe of securities is only mentioned to the extent that it includes *a*, *b*, and *c*, so that the same conclusion will apply in any universe which includes these securities.

APPENDIX

An alternative to the basic premise that security prices are arbitrage-free is that they are prices at which all planned purchases and sales of securities are consistent, that is, are equilibrium prices.

In this paradigm there is a given number of securities and a given number of agents. Each agent has some given initial portfolio and some given preferences. These preferences take the form of the specification of which portfolio of any pair of portfolios the agent prefers, or of his being indifferent between the two. Since a portfolio specifies (positive or negative) receipts on various dates and states such preferences are equivalent to preferences over receipts on various dates and states. They thus embody views of the likelihood of various states, or probabilities, as well as measures of impatience and risk aversion.

Preferences are assumed to satisfy certain regularity conditions. The most basic of these is that if one portfolio specifies at least as large a receipt as a second portfolio on each date and state and a larger receipt on some then the first portfolio is preferred to the second.

Given a system of prices each agent plans purchases and sales of securities. The resulting planned portfolio, that is, the agent's initial portfolio plus his net planned purchases, must be feasible, in that its cost at the given prices must not exceed the cost of his initial portfolio. It must also be best, in that the agent must prefer it to any other feasible portfolio.

There is no guarantee that there is a best portfolio. However, if there is, then the given prices are arbitrage-free prices. This is because if there were some arbitrage portfolio at these prices then the agent could feasibly add this arbitrage portfolio to his best portfolio, since the arbitrage portfolio is costless, and this addition would produce a portfolio which the agent prefers to his best portfolio, since the arbitrage portfolio involves negative receipts on no dates or states and positive receipts on some.

Equilibrium prices are prices at which the sum of all agents' planned purchases of each security is equal to the corresponding sum of planned sales. Equivalently, they are prices at which aggregate planned portfolios are equal to aggregate initial portfolios. If the given prices are equilibrium prices then all planned purchases and sales are consistent and will be effected, so that planned and actual portfolios will become the same.

Even if all agents have best portfolios at all given prices there is no guarantee that equilibrium prices exist. Indeed, even with strong regularity conditions on agents' preferences, there may be no equilibrium prices (see Allingham, 1989). If there are no equilibrium prices then the equilibrium paradigm is vacuous.

If there are some equilibrium prices these, unlike arbitrage-free prices, will depend on the enumeration of the securities and of the agents. If a new security is added then in general each agent's planned purchases and sales of other securities will change, and if a new agent is added then in general total planned purchases and sales of all securities will change. In either case these changes will imply a change in equilibrium prices.

Since agents have best portfolios at equilibrium prices and the existence of best portfolios implies the absence of arbitrage it follows that equilibrium prices are arbitrage-free prices. However, arbitrage-free prices may not be equilibrium prices. Equilibrium prices depend on agents' preferences and initial portfolios while arbitrage prices do not. There will then typically be a number of arbitrage-free prices, only some of which will be equilibrium prices for any particular configuration of preferences and initial portfolios.

Thus the concept of arbitrage-free prices requires data only on securities but makes only general restrictions on security prices, while the concept of equilibrium prices further requires (typically unobservable) data on agents but makes correspondingly more specific restrictions. However, as is shown in the appendix to Chapter 2, the premise that security prices are equilibrium prices in itself, that is, with no specific information on preferences and initial portfolios, implies no more restrictions than does the premise that security prices are arbitrage-free prices.

BIBLIOGRAPHY

Allingham, M. (1989) *Theory of Markets* (London: Macmillan).

International Stock Exchange (1990) 'International Stock Exchange Comparisons', *Quality of Markets Quarterly Review*, Spring, pp. 22–9.

Jarrow R. (1988) *Finance Theory* (Englewood Cliffs: Prentice-Hall).

Ross S. A. (1989) 'Finance' in J. Eatwell, M. Milgate and P. Newman (eds) *The New Palgrave: Finance* (London: Macmillan).

2 The Basic Arbitrage Theorem

This chapter formalises some of the concepts introduced in Chapter 1 and uses these to establish the basic arbitrage theorem, that in the absence of arbitrage security prices may be expressed as expected discounted values.

ARBITRAGE PORTFOLIOS

We assume there to be m possible states, identified by the (superscript) index

$$k = 1, \ldots, m.$$

A random variable x is a variable which may take a different value in each state; it is represented by a list, or vector, of its possible values, that is by

$$(x^1, \ldots, x^m)$$

where x^k is its value in state k.

Operations on one, or more, random variables are applied to the values of the variable, or variables, in each state; thus, for example, $\sqrt{x}$ is the list

$$(\sqrt{x^1}, \ldots, \sqrt{x^m})$$

and $x + y$ is the list

$$(x^1 + y^1, \ldots, x^m + y^m).$$

Similarly, relations between random variables apply to the values of the variables in each state, so that, for example

$$x = y$$

implies that

$$x^k = y^k$$

for each state k. (The exceptions to this rule are that

$$x > y$$

implies that

$$x^k \geqslant y^k$$

for each state k with

$$x^k > y^k$$

for some, and that

$$x < y$$

has an analogous implication).

We commence by considering the single-period case where there are two dates, labelled 0 and 1. We consider n securities, identified by the (subscript) index

$$i = 1, \ldots, n.$$

Security i is identified by its payoff on date 1, that is by the random variable x_i. It is a limited liability security if

$$x_i > 0,$$

that is to say if its payoff is semi-positive. We assume that there is some limited liability security.

A portfolio is a list of holdings of securities, say

$$a = (a_1, \ldots, a_n)$$

where a_i is the holding of security i. The payoff x_a of this portfolio is the sum of the payoffs of its constituents, that is

$$x_a = \sum_i a_i x_i.$$

A price system is a list of security prices, say

$$p = (p_1, \ldots, p_n),$$

where p_i is the price of security i. The cost p_a of a portfolio at these prices is the sum of the costs of its constituents, that is

$$p_a = \sum_i p_i a_i,$$

which inner product is written as *p.a.*

An arbitrage portfolio at the prices p is a limited liability portfolio whose cost at these prices is non-positive, that is, a portfolio a such that

$$p_a \leqslant 0$$

and

$$x_a > 0.$$

Thus in the absence of arbitrage

$$x_a > 0$$

implies that

$$p_a > 0.$$

For example, if security 1, say, is a limited liability security and

$$a = (1, 0, \ldots, 0)$$

then

$$x_a = x_1 > 0$$

so that

$$p_a = p_1 > 0.$$

Thus in the absence of arbitrage the price of a limited liability security is positive.

If a is a limited liability portfolio with zero cost then it is a limited liability portfolio with non-positive cost. Further, assume that a is a limited liability portfolio with non-positive cost and that security 1 has limited liability, and let

$$b = (a_1 + \varepsilon, \, a_2, \, \ldots, a_n)$$

where

$$\varepsilon = -p.a/p_1 \geqslant 0.$$

Then

$$p_b = p.b = p.a - p.a = 0$$

and

$$x_b = x_a + \varepsilon x_1 > 0,$$

so that b is a limited liability portfolio with zero cost. Thus the existence of an arbitrage portfolio at the prices p is equivalent to the existence of a limited liability portfolio whose cost at these prices is zero.

Arbitrage-free prices are prices at which there is no arbitrage portfolio, or equivalently at which there is no zero-cost limited liability portfolio. A constructive demonstration of the existence of such prices is straightforward. Let

$$p_i = \sum{}^k x_i{}^k$$

for each security i. Then if a is an arbitrage portfolio at the prices p

$$p.a = \sum_i \left(\sum^k x_i^k a_i \right) = \sum^k \left(\sum_i x_i^k a_i \right) \leqslant 0$$

and

$$\sum_i x_i^k a_i \geqslant 0$$

for each state k with

$$\sum_i x_i^k a_i > 0$$

for some. But the latter conditions imply that

$$\sum^k \sum_i x_i^k a_i > 0,$$

which contradicts the former. It follows that there can be no arbitrage portfolio, so that p is an arbitrage-free price system. Thus there are always some arbitrage-free prices; indeed, there may be many.

Consider the example with two states and two securities with the payoffs

$$x_1 = (1, 4)$$

$$x_2 = (2, 3).$$

As both securities have limited liability the arbitrage-free prices of each are positive. If a is a (zero-cost) arbitrage portfolio at the prices p then

$$p_1 a_1 + p_2 a_2 = 0$$

and

$$a_1 + 2a_2 \geqslant 0$$

$$4a_1 + 3a_2 \geqslant 0,$$

with one of the inequalities strict. If a_1 is zero then a_2 must be zero or the cost will not be zero, and this zero portfolio is not an arbitrage portfolio. Thus

$$p_1/p_2 = -a_2/a_1,$$

and if a_1 is positive then

$$-a_2/a_1 \leqslant 0.50$$

$$-a_2/a_1 \leqslant 1.33,$$

so that

$$p_1/p_2 \leqslant 0.50.$$

Similarly, if a_1 is negative then

$$p_1/p_2 \geqslant 1.33.$$

Thus there will be no arbitrage if neither of these conditions holds, which is to say that arbitrage-free prices are any positive prices p such that

$$0.50 < p_1/p_2 < 1.33.$$

STATE PRICES

If there is, for each state k, a security with unit payoff in state k and zero payoff in all other states, that is, a basis security for state k, then the price of this security, say q^k, may be interpreted as a state price for k. As basis securities have limited liability their arbitrage-free prices are positive. Further, any security may be replicated by a portfolio of basis securities. For example, security i has the same payoff as does a portfolio consisting of, for each state k, x_i^k units of the basis security for state k. Then in the absence of arbitrage the cost of security i is the same as the cost of this portfolio, which is to say that

$$p_i = \sum\nolimits^k q^k x_i{}^k = q.x_i$$

for each security i.

This result, with q interpreted as implicit state prices, applies whether or not basis securities exist. That is, the absence of an arbitrage portfolio at the prices p is equivalent to the existence of some positive implicit state prices q such that

$$p_i = q.x_i$$

for each security i.

To demonstrate that the existence of some positive state prices q implies the absence of arbitrage suppose that a is an arbitrage portfolio at p. Then

$$p.a = \sum\nolimits_i (q.x_i)a_i = q.(\sum\nolimits_i a_i x_i) = q.x_a \leqslant 0$$

and

$$x_a > 0.$$

Since this is impossible with q positive there can be no arbitrage portfolio a.

To demonstrate that the absence of arbitrage implies the existence of some positive state prices q assume that there are no arbitrage portfolios and consider the set of all payoffs which can be obtained at zero cost, that is, the set of all payoffs y such that, for some portfolio a,

$$p.a = 0$$

and

$$x_a = y.$$

This set contains all linear combinations of its elements. Specifically, if it contains y (say with the corresponding portfolio a) then it contains αy for any number α (with the corresponding portfolio αa), and if it contains y and z (say with the corresponding portfolios a and b respectively) then it contains $y+z$ (with the corresponding portfolio $a+b$). In particular, it contains the zero payoff. However, it contains no semi-positive payoff: if it did then the corresponding portfolio would be an arbitrage portfolio.

Then it follows from the separating hyperplane theorem (see Lancaster, 1968; R4.3) that there is some positive vector q such that

$$q.y=0$$

for all payoffs y in the set, or equivalently

$$q.x_a = q.(\textstyle\sum_i a_i x_i) = \sum_i (q.x_i)a_i = 0$$

for all portfolios a such that

$$p.a = \textstyle\sum_i p_i a_i = 0.$$

This implies that

$$p_i = q.x_i$$

for each security i, as required.

This argument does not imply that state prices are unique. Consider the example where there are two states and one security whose payoff is

$$x_1 = (1, 4)$$

and whose price is unity. Then q will be a vector of state prices if q is positive and

$$q^1 + 4q^2 = 1.$$

It is clear that there are many state prices. Now add a second security whose payoff is

$$x_2 = (2, 3)$$

and whose price is also unity. This is now the example discussed above, where arbitrage-free prices are any positive prices p such that

$$0.50 < p_1/p_2 < 1.33;$$

clearly the present prices are arbitrage-free. Now q will be a vector of state prices if q is positive and

$$q^1 + 4q^2 = 1$$
$$2q^1 + 3q^2 = 1,$$

that is, if

$$q^1 = q^2 = 0.2.$$

In this case state prices are unique.

The relevance of state prices is that they allow the valuation of other securities. The unique arbitrage-free price of some third security with the payoff

$$x^3 = (5, 5)$$

is given directly by the state prices as

$$5q^1 + 5q^2 = 2.$$

THE MARTINGALE PROPERTY

State prices may be interpreted as the product of a discount factor and some probabilities such that security prices are expected discounted payoffs. More precisely, there is an implicit discount factor δ and some shadow, or martingale, probabilities

$$\pi = (\pi^1, \ldots, \pi^m),$$

where π^k is the martingale probability of state k occurring, such that arbitrage-free security prices p are expected discounted payoffs. That is, δ and π are such that

$$p_i = \sum{}^k \pi^k \delta x_i{}^k = \hat{E}\delta x_i = \delta \hat{E}x_i$$

for each security i where $\hat{E}$ is the expectation operator under the martingale probabilities π.

If there is some risk-free security, say security 1, then

$$p_1 = \delta \hat{E}x_1 = \delta x_1$$

so that

$$\delta = p_1/x_1 > 0$$

is the risk-free discount factor. Equivalently

$$\rho = (x_1 - p_1)/p_1 = 1/\delta - 1$$

is the risk-free interest rate.

If there are some state prices q the discount factor may be defined by

$$\delta = \sum{}^k q^k > 0$$

and the probabilities by

$$\pi = q/\sum{}^k q^k.$$

The probabilities π are positive, since q is positive, and their sum is unity, since

$$\sum{}^k \pi^k = \sum{}^k q^k / \sum{}^k q^k = 1.$$

Conversely, if there is a discount factor δ and some shadow probabilities π then state prices may be defined by

$q = \delta\pi.$

It follows that the existence of such a discount factor and probabilities is equivalent to the existence of some state prices.

Since the absence of arbitrage is equivalent to the existence of state prices, which in turn is equivalent to the existence of some appropriate discount factor and martingale probabilities, we have the basic arbitrage theorem: the absence of arbitrage is equivalent to the martingale property, that security prices may be expressed as expected discounted values.

Returning to the example where security payoffs are given by

$$x_1 = (1, 4)$$

$$x_2 = (2, 3)$$

$$x_3 = (5, 5),$$

security prices by

$$p = (1, 1, 2)$$

and state prices by

$$q = (0.2, 0.2)$$

we have

$$\delta = p_3/x_3 = 0.4$$

and

$$\pi = q/\delta = (0.5, 0.5).$$

Thus the discount factor is 0.4, or equivalently the interest rate is 1.5, and the shadow probability of each state is 0.5.

MANY PERIODS

The basic arbitrage theorem is immediately extended to the many-period setting by applying it in each period in turn, commencing with the last. We consider s periods, or $s+1$ dates, and identify these dates by the index

$$t = 0, \ldots, s.$$

The evolution of states k over time is represented by the nodal structure of states, as illustrated in Figure 2.1.

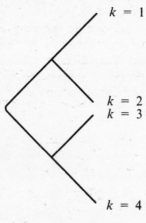

Figure 2.1

   The value of a security at any node on date s is simply the dollar payoff of the security on date s in the state (or set of states) corresponding to the node. Then at any node on date $s-1$ there is a discount factor and some (conditional) martingale probabilities such that the value of the security at the node (before any payoff on date s is made) is the expected discounted value of the payoffs at the succeeding nodes, that is at the nodes on date s which lie on a path through the given node. Similarly, at any node on date $s-2$

there is a discount factor and some (conditional) martingale probabilities such that the value of the security at the node (before any payoff on date $s-1$ is made) is the expected discounted value of the payoffs at the succeeding nodes, where the payoff at any such node is interpreted as the value at that node plus any dollar payoff on date $s-1$ in the set of states corresponding to that node.

Repeating this recursive procedure a further $s-2$ times determines the value for the security on date 0, that is the current price of the security.

Equivalently, an overall discount factor for each state may be defined as the product of the discount factors in each period for the state, and an overall martingale probability for each state may be defined as the product of the relevant conditional martingale probabilities.

Given some state k we denote the node on date t for this state by $v^k(t)$, and (if t is prior to s) denote the discount factor and conditional martingale probability of state k at the node $v^k(t)$ by $\delta^k(t)$ and $\pi^k(t)$ respectively. Then the overall discount factor and martingale probability for state k are the products

$$\delta^k = \delta^k(0). \ . \ .\delta^k(s-1)$$

and

$$\pi^k = \pi^k(0) \ . \ . \ . \ \pi^k(s-1)$$

respectively.

Consider a security i whose dollar payoff x_i occurs on date s only. This involves no loss of generality since a security with dollar payoffs on dates t and s may be considered to consist of two securities: one with a payoff on date t only and one with a payoff on date s only. Applying the martingale property to this security we have

$$p_i = \hat{E}\delta x_i$$

where δ is the overall discount factor and $\hat{E}$ the martingale expectation operator, so that the price of the security is given by its expected discounted payoff (under the martingale probabilities). In general, we do not have

$$\hat{E}\delta x_i = (\hat{E}\delta)(\hat{E}x_i),$$

so that the price of the security is not given by its expected payoff discounted at the expected discount factor. However, this property does obtain if discount factors and payoffs are independent (under the martingale probabilities), for example, because either one is deterministic.

If discount factors are deterministic, in that for each date t

$$\delta^k(t) = \delta(t),$$

say, for each state k, then

$$\delta^k = \delta(0) \ldots \delta(s-1) = \delta,$$

say, for each state k, so that

$$p_i = \hat{E}\delta x_i = \delta\hat{E}x_i,$$

and the security price is the discounted expected payoff (under the martingale probabilities). Similarly, if payoffs are deterministic then

$$p_i = \hat{E}\delta x_i = x_i\hat{E}\delta,$$

and the security price is the payoff discounted at the expected discount rate (again under the martingale probabilities).

The relevance of the martingale property in a many-period setting is the same as that in a single-period setting: the prices and payoffs of some given securities determine the structure of discount factors and martingale probabilities, which in turn determine the prices of other securities.

Consider the example where the nodal structure of states is that illustrated in Figure 2.1. Discount factors on each date and state are given, being those illustrated in Figure 2.2. There are three securities whose payoffs on date 2 in the four states are

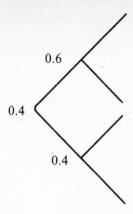

Figure 2.2

(10, 10, 10, 10)

(10, 20, 20, 10)

(60, 40, 40, 10).

The prices of these three securities are 2, 3, and 8 respectively.

The martingale probability of states 1 or 2 occurring is denoted by α; the conditional martingale probability of state 1 occurring given that states 1 or 2 are possible is denoted by β; and the conditional martingale probability of state 3 occurring given that states 3 or 4 are possible is denoted by γ. Applying the martingale property for the three securities gives

$$2 = 0.4\big[0.6\alpha[10\beta + 10(1-\beta)] + 0.4(1-\alpha)[10\gamma + 10(1-\gamma)]\big]$$

$$3 = 0.4\big[0.6\alpha[10\beta + 20(1-\beta)] + 0.4(1-\alpha)[20\gamma + 10(1-\gamma)]\big]$$

$$8 = 0.4\big[0.6\alpha[60\beta + 40(1-\beta)] + 0.4(1-\alpha)[40\gamma + 10(1-\gamma)]\big]$$

respectively. Solving these three equations gives

Arbitrage

$\alpha = \beta = \gamma = 0.5,$

so that the three probabilities are 0.5.

Equivalently, the overall discount factors in and martingale probabilities of the four states are

(0.24, 0.24, 0.16, 0.16)

and

(0.25, 0.25, 0.25, 0.25)

respectively.

In this example there are three nodes prior to date s and thus three independent probabilities; given the corresponding three discount factors these probabilities are determined by the prices and payoffs of three (independent) securities. If discount factors are not given then discount factors and martingale probabilities are determined jointly by the martingale property, but now six (independent) securities are required.

For example, if discount factors are not given but there are three further securities whose payoffs on date 2 in the four states are

(50, 40, 30, 20)

(20, 30, 40, 50)

(40, 30, 40, 30)

and whose prices are 7.4, 6.6 and 7.0 respectively then discount factors and martingale probabilities are jointly determined by the martingale property as those specified above.

More generally, if there are h nodes prior to date s then all discount factors and martingale probabilities are determined by the prices and payoffs of $2h$ (independent) securities.

Now consider a security i whose payoff in the four states is

(30, 10, 10, 0).

The price of this security is determined recursively as follows. At the node on date 1 at which the discount factor is 0.6 the value of the security is given by the martingale property as 12, and at the node on date 1 at which the discount factor is 0.4 the value of the security is given as 2. Then using these values for date 1 the value of the security on date 0, that is, the current price of the security, is given as

$p_i = 2.8.$

The structure of security prices is thus that illustrated in Figure 2.3.

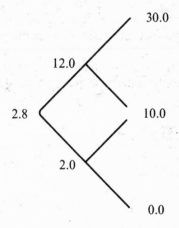

Figure 2.3

Equivalently, the price of the security is determined directly by the overall discount factors and martingale probabilities as

$\hat{E}\delta x_i = 2.8 = p_i.$

In this example

$$\hat{E}\delta = 0.2$$

and

$$\hat{E}x_i = 12.5$$

so that

$$(\hat{E}\delta)(\hat{E}x_i) = 2.5 < p_i.$$

Thus, as discount factors and payoffs are not independent, the price of the security is not given by its expected payoff discounted at the expected discount rate (under the martingale probabilities).

CORPORATE SECURITIES

A simple application of the basic arbitrage theorem involves the pricing of corporate securities. A company is financed by debt with a (positive) nominal value of θ and by equity. At the end of the period the company will liquidate its assets and distribute the proceeds, x_c. We consider the relation between the price of the company's debt, p_d, and the price of its equity, p_e.

If x_c is less than θ then debt holders receive x_c and equity holders receive zero, while if x_c is greater than θ then debt holders receive θ and equity holders receive the remainder. Thus the payoff of debt, which is assumed to be semi-positive, is

$$x_d = \min(x_c, \theta)$$

and that of equity, which is also assumed to be semi-positive, is

$$x_e = \max(x_c - \theta, 0)$$

so that

$$x_d + x_e = x_c.$$

Applying the martingale property we have

$$p_d = \delta\hat{E}x_d$$

and

$$p_e = \delta\hat{E}x_e$$

where δ is a discount factor and $\hat{E}$ the martingale expectation operator. Then

$$p_d + p_e = \delta\hat{E}x_d + \delta\hat{E}x_e = \delta\hat{E}(x_d + x_e) = \delta\hat{E}x_c.$$

Since δ, $\hat{E}$ and x_c are independent of θ it follows that the sum of debt and equity prices is a constant which is independent of the nominal value of debt. Further, the gearing of the company, that is

$$\gamma = p_d/(p_d + p_e),$$

which is well-defined since both p_d and p_e are positive as both payoffs are semi-positive, is completely defined by θ. Thus the sum of debt and equity prices, or equivalently the price of the company, p_c, is independent of gearing.

This result is known as the Modigliani–Miller irrelevancy proposition (see Modigliani and Miller, 1958). A more direct demonstration of this result is as follows. Consider the strategy of buying the company and selling both debt and equity. The payoff of this strategy is

$$x_c - x_d - x_e = 0,$$

so that the cost, which is

$$p_c - p_d - p_e,$$

must also be zero. This implies that

$$p_c = p_d + p_e.$$

Since this applies for all levels of γ it follows that p_c is independent of γ.

Given some arbitrary probabilities the expected (rate of) return of debt is

$$Er_d = Ex_d/p_d - 1$$

and that of equity is

$$Er_e = Ex_e/p_e - 1$$

where E is the expectation operator under these arbitrary probabilities. The expected return of the company is

$$Er_c = Ex_c/p_c - 1.$$

Equivalently, the expected return of the company is the value-weighted average of the expected returns of debt and equity, since

$$(p_d Er_d + p_e Er_e)/(p_d + p_e) = (Ex_d + Ex_e)/p_c - 1$$

$$= E(x_d + x_e)/p_c - 1$$

$$= Ex_c/p_c - 1.$$

Then as p_c is independent of gearing the expected return of the company is also independent of gearing. This conclusion contrasts with the 'traditional' theory of corporate finance which asserts that the expected return of the company, which is interpreted as the cost of capital, at first decreases and then increases as gearing rises, so that there is some non-trivial least-cost gearing ratio (see Modigliani and Miller, 1958).

EVIDENCE

The irrelevancy proposition may be tested by examining the relation between expected return, Er_c, and gearing, γ. This is best investigated by examining a cross-section of companies whose expected returns in any given state are similar. Such a class of companies, or risk class, may be approximated by an industrial grouping.

A problem with such tests is that expected returns are not observable. This problem may be resolved either by representing expected returns by realised returns, or by employing some market model which relates expected returns to other factors.

The first approach involves estimating the parameters α and β of the equation

$$r_c = \alpha + \beta\gamma$$

where r_c is the realised return. The irrelevancy proposition implies that there will be no significant relationship between the variables r_c and γ.

These parameters, and associated statistics, are estimated using the statistical technique of (ordinary least squares) regression (see Johnston, 1984; 2.2, 5.3). This procedure produces best estimates of the values of the parameters together with their corresponding t-statistics. The t-statistic of a parameter, that is, the ratio of the best estimate of the parameter to the standard deviation of this estimate, measures the statistical significance of the parameter; approximately, a parameter differs from zero with 0.95 probability if its t-statistic exceeds 2 (see Johnston, 1984; 2.5, 5.4). The procedure also produces an estimate of the correlation between the two variables (see Johnston, 1984; 2.3).

This approach is applied by Modigliani and Miller (1958) to two risk classes. The estimated coefficients, with returns expressed as annual percentages, together with t-statistics for the gearing coefficient β and correlations, are given in Table 2.1. In each class the coefficient β is not significantly different from zero, and the correlation is negligible. The coefficients α, which measure the means of r_c, accord with expectations.

Table   2.1

α	β	*t-statistic*	*Correlation*
0.053	0.006	0.8	0.12
0.085	0.006	0.3	0.04

The second approach assumes that within any risk class the expected return of the company is given by

$$Er_c = \rho + \beta_c(Er_a - \rho)$$

and the expected return of equity by

$$Er_e = \rho + \beta_e(Er_a - \rho)$$

where ρ is the risk-free interest rate, r_a the expected return on some market index, and β_c and β_e the ratios of the covariances of r_c and r_e respectively with r_a to the variance of r_a. (The rationale for this assumption is discussed in Chapter 3.)

Using this approach the irrelevancy proposition is tested by estimating the relevant covariances and variance from a time-series sample and comparing the standard deviations of β_c and β_e obtained from these estimates. Within any risk class the values of r_c, and thus, as ρ and r_a are the same for all companies, of β_c, will be approximately equal. But the values of r_e, and thus of β_e, will be more diverse, since these will depend on γ, which will vary within each risk class. Thus the irrelevancy proposition implies that the standard deviation of β_c will be less than that of β_e.

This approach is applied by Hamada (1972) to nine risk classes. In eight of the nine classes the standard deviation of β_c is less than that of β_e, an outcome which, if there were no systematic relation between the two, would have a probability of less than 0.02; in the remaining class the difference is insignificant.

APPENDIX

The result that equilibrium prices are arbitrage-free may be confirmed more formally as follows. Each agent prefers portfolio b to portfolio c if the payoff of b is at least as large as that of c in all states and larger in some, that is, if

$$x_b > x_c.$$

If p is a system of equilibrium prices then some agent has a best portfolio, b, at these prices. Then, if the agent's initial portfolio is g the cost of b does not exceed the cost of g, that is

$$p.b \leqslant p.g.$$

Also, there is no portfolio whose cost does not exceed that of g which the agent prefers to b; thus there is no portfolio c such that

$$p.c \leqslant p.g$$

and

$$x_c > x_b.$$

Now suppose that a is an arbitrage portfolio at the prices p, that is,

$$p.a \leqslant 0$$

and

$$x_a > 0,$$

and let

$$c = b + a.$$

Then

$$p.c = p.b + p.a \leqslant p.g$$

and

$$x_c = x_b + x_a > x_b,$$

which is inconsistent with b being a best portfolio. It follows that there is no arbitrage portfolio, and thus that the equilibrium prices p are arbitrage-free.

While arbitrage-free prices may not be equilibrium prices for all configurations of agents' preferences and initial portfolios they are equilibrium prices for some such configuration. To confirm this we show, with no loss of generality, that any arbitrage-free prices are equilibrium prices for some particularly simple configuration.

Assume that p is an arbitrage-free system of prices and δ and π some corresponding discount factor and martingale probabilities. Then let each agent's initial portfolio be zero, and specify that each agent prefers the portfolio b to the portfolio c if

$$u(b) > u(c)$$

where u is a (utility) function defined by

$$u(a) = -\sum^k \pi^k \exp(-\sum_i x_i^k a_i),$$

exp being the exponential function defined by

$$\exp(\alpha) = 1 + \alpha + \alpha^2/2 + \alpha^3/6 \ldots$$

To confirm that this specification of preferences is valid assume that

$$x_b > x_c.$$

Then

$$\sum_i x_i^k b_i \geqslant \sum_i x_i^k c_i$$

so that

$$-\pi^k \exp(-\sum_i x_i^k b_i) \geqslant -\pi^k \exp(-\sum_i x_i^k c_i)$$

for all states k with strict inequality for some, from which it follows that

$$u(b) > u(c),$$

as required.

Each agent's best portfolio is the portfolio which maximises $u(a)$ subject to

$$p.a \leqslant 0.$$

Suppose that $p.a$ is negative and, without loss of generality, that security 1 has limited liability, and let

$$b = (a_1 + \varepsilon, a_2, \ldots, a_n)$$

where

$$\varepsilon = -p.a/p_1 > 0.$$

Then

$$p.b = 0$$

and

$$u(b) > u(a)$$

as security 1 has limited liability. It follows that $p.a$ cannot be negative, so that each agent's best portfolio is the portfolio which maximises $u(a)$ subject to

$$v(a) = p.a = 0.$$

It follows from the Lagrangean theorem (see Lancaster, 1968; 4.2, 4.5) that this maximisation problem has a unique solution characterised by

$$\partial u(a)/\partial a_i = \lambda \partial v(a)/\partial a_i$$

for each security i where λ is a constant, and where $\partial u(a)/\partial a_i$ is the derivative of $u(a)$ with respect to a_i, and so forth (see Lancaster; 1968, R8.2). Applying this result, and noting that

$$\partial \exp(\alpha)/\partial \alpha = 1 + \alpha + \alpha^2/2 + \alpha^3/6 + \ldots = \exp(\alpha),$$

we have

$$\sum\nolimits^k \pi^k x_i^k \exp(-\sum\nolimits_i x_i^k a_i) = \lambda p_i$$

for each security i. This condition will be satisfied if a is zero, for then

$$\exp(-\sum\nolimits_i x_i^k a_i) = \exp(0) = 1$$

for each state k, so that

$$\sum\nolimits^k \pi^k x_i^k \exp(-\sum\nolimits_i x_i^k a_i) = \sum\nolimits^k \pi^k x_i^k = p_i/\delta,$$

and the maximisation condition holds for

$$\lambda = 1/\delta.$$

It follows that the zero portfolio is the solution of the maximisation problem.

Thus at the prices p each agent's best portfolio is the same as his initial portfolio, so that his planned purchases and sales of all securities are zero. It follows that total planned purchases are the same as total planned sales for each security, and thus that p is an equilibrium price.

The relevance of this result, that arbitrage-free prices are equilibrium prices for some configuration of agents' preferences and initial portfolios, is that the premise that security prices are equilibrium prices in itself, that is with no specific information on preferences or initial portfolios, implies no more than does the premise that security prices are arbitrage-free prices.

Martingale probabilities in an equilibrium framework may be interpreted as probabilities at which markets consisting of risk-neutral agents are in equilibrium. An agent is risk-neutral if he evaluates portfolios solely on the basis of their expected payoffs. Given some arbitrary probabilities such an agent may be considered to have the utility function w defined by

$$w(a) = Ex_a = \sum_i a_i Ex_i$$

where E is the expectation operator under these arbitrary probabilities.

The portfolio which maximises $w(a)$ subject to

$$v(a) = p.a = 0$$

is characterised by

$$\partial w(a)/\partial a_i = Ex_i = \lambda \partial v(a)/\partial a_i = \lambda p_i$$

for each security i where λ is a constant, or equivalently by

$$p_i = \delta Ex_i$$

for each security i where

$$\delta = 1/\lambda.$$

This condition is the same as the martingale property

$$p_i = \delta \hat{E}x_i$$

for each security i when the martingale probabilities, under which the expectation operator $\hat{E}$ is applied, are the same as the arbitrary probabilities, under which the expectation operator E is applied. Thus martingale probabilities are the probabilities at which markets consisting of risk-neutral agents are in equilibrium.

BIBLIOGRAPHY

Dybvig, P. H. and Ross, S. A. (1989) 'Arbitrage', J. Eatwell, M. Milgate and P. Newman (eds), *The New Palgrave: Finance* (London: Macmillan).

Hamada, R. (1972) 'The Effect of the Firm's Capital Structure on the Systematic Risk of Common Stocks', *Journal of Finance*, no 27, pp. 435–52.

Harrison, J. and Kreps, D. (1979) 'Martingales and Arbitrage in Multiperiod Securities Markets', *Journal of Economic Theory*, no 20, pp. 381–408.

Johnston, J. (1984) *Econometric Methods* (New York: McGraw-Hill) 3rd edn.

Lancaster, K. (1968) *Mathematical Economics* (Toronto: Macmillan).

Modigliani, F. and Miller, M. (1958) 'The Cost of Capital, Corporation Finance, and the Theory of Investment', *American Economic Review*, no 48, pp. 261–97.

Ross, S. (1978) 'A Simple Approach to the Valuation of Risky Streams', *Journal of Business*, no 51, pp. 453–75.

Rubinstein, M. (1987) 'Derivative Asset Analysis', *Journal of Economic Perspectives*, no 1, pp. 73–93.

Varian, H. R. (1987) 'The Arbitrage Principle in Financial Economics', *Journal of Economic Perspectives*, no 1, pp. 55–72.

Part II
A Single Period

3 Exact Arbitrage: A Capital Asset Pricing Model

This chapter applies the basic arbitrage theorem in a single-period setting to develop a version of what is known as the capital asset pricing model (or CAPM).

A PRICING RELATION

The CAPM assumes that there are some agents whose holdings of securities do not depend on security prices. The aggregate short holdings of such agents, or equivalently the aggregate long holdings of all other agents, is known as the market portfolio.

Given the existence of a meaningful (positive and risky) market portfolio the CAPM assumes that payoffs of securities in some given units of value are linear functions of the payoff of this market portfolio. Then the payoff of security i is

$$x_i = \alpha_i + \gamma_i x_a$$

where α_i and γ_i are constants and x_a is the payoff of the market portfolio a.

Given some arbitrary probabilities the payoff of security i may be written as

$$x_i = Ex_i + \gamma_i(x_a - Ex_a)$$

where E is the expectation operator under these probabilities.

Since the covariance of x_i with x_a is

$$\text{cov}(x_i, x_a) = \text{E}(x_i - \text{E}x_i)(x_a - \text{E}x_a)$$

$$= \text{E}\gamma_i(x_a - \text{E}x_a)^2$$

$$= \gamma_i \text{E}(x_a - \text{E}x_a)^2$$

$$= \gamma_i \text{var}(x_a)$$

where $\text{var}(x_a)$ is the variance of x_a, the parameter γ_i is given by

$$\gamma_i = \text{cov}(x_i, x_a)/\text{var}(x_a).$$

As this linear payoff relation applies for all securities it also applies for all linear combinations of securities, that is, for all portfolios. Thus if b is a portfolio then

$$x_b = \sum_i b_i x_i = \alpha_b + \gamma_b x_a.$$

Since

$$\text{cov}(x_b, x_a) = \text{cov}(\sum_i b_i x_i, x_a) = \sum_i b_i \text{cov}(x_i, x_a)$$

we have

$$\gamma_b = \sum_i b_i \text{cov}(x_i, x_a)/\text{var}(x_a) = \sum_i b_i \gamma_i = b.\gamma.$$

In particular, for the portfolio a we have

$$\gamma_a = \text{cov}(x_a, x_a)/\text{var}(x_a) = \text{var}(x_a)/\text{var}(x_a) = 1.$$

Choose some portfolio b such that

$$\alpha_b = \sum_i b_i \alpha_i > 0$$

and

$$\gamma_b = \sum_i b_i \gamma_i = 0.$$

It follows from the solution theorem for homogeneous equations (see Lancaster, 1968; R3.3) that such a choice is possible as only two homogeneous restrictions are imposed on the n portfolio quantities. Then

$$x_b = \alpha_b > 0,$$

so that b is a risk-free portfolio.

Applying the martingale property we have

$$p_i = \delta \hat{E} x_i$$

for each security i where δ is a discount factor and $\hat{E}$ the martingale expectation operator. We then have the pricing relation

$$p_i = \delta E x_i + \gamma_i(\delta \hat{E} x_a - \delta E x_a) = \delta E x_i - \gamma_i(\delta E x_a - p_a)$$

for each security (or portfolio) i where

$$p_a = \delta \hat{E} x_a$$

is the price of the market portfolio a.

This pricing relation gives the price of security i as its discounted expected payoff $\delta E x_i$ minus a risk element equal to the product of γ_i and

$$\delta E x_a - p_a = \delta(E x_a - \hat{E} x_a).$$

The first term in this product is the sensitivity of the payoff of the security to the payoff of the market portfolio. The second term is the discounted expected gain of the market portfolio, or equivalently the risk premium associated with the market portfolio.

We thus have

$$p_i = \delta E x_i - (\delta E x_a - p_a) \operatorname{cov}(x_i, x_a)/\operatorname{var}(x_a),$$

or equivalently

$$\delta Ex_i - p_i = \text{cov}(x_i, x_a)(\delta Ex_a - p_a)/\text{var}(x_a),$$

for each security i, so that the discounted expected gain of a security is proportional to the covariance of the payoff of the security with that of the market portfolio, the constant of proportionality being the discounted expected gain of the market portfolio per unit of its variance.

UNITS OF VALUE

Assume that the linear payoff relations

$$x_i = \alpha_i + \gamma_i x_a$$

apply when payoffs are denominated in dollars, and let z be the sterling–dollar, say, exchange rate. Then denoting the sterling payoffs of security i and of the market portfolio by

$$y_i = x_i z$$

and

$$y_a = x_a z$$

respectively we have

$$y_i = \alpha_i z + \gamma_i y_a$$

for each security i. Unless z is constant the sterling payoff of security i is not a linear function of the sterling market payoff. It follows that the linear payoff assumption of the CAPM is not independent of the units of value in which securities are measured.

The sterling payoff relation may also be written as

$$y_i = (Ey_i/Ez)z + \gamma_i[y_a - (Ey_a/Ez)z]$$

for each security i, noting that the exchange rate, and thus

Ez, is positive. Then applying the martingale property we have the sterling pricing relations

$$q_i = \varepsilon E y_i - \gamma_i(q_a - \varepsilon E y_a)$$

for each security i where q_i and q_a are sterling prices and

$$\varepsilon = \delta \hat{E} z / E z.$$

The constant ε may be interpreted as the dollar discount rate multiplied by the currency risk factor, that is, by the ratio of the expectation of the exchange rate under the martingale probabilities to this expectation under the given arbitrary probabilities. The constant γ_i is given by

$$\gamma_i = \text{cov}(y_i - \alpha_i z, y_a)/\text{var}(y_a)$$

$$= \text{cov}(y_i, y_a)/\text{var}(y_a) - \alpha_i \text{cov}(z, y_a)/\text{var}(y_a).$$

Now assume that the exchange rate and the sterling market payoff, or equivalently the exchange rate and the dollar market payoff, are independent. Then

$$\text{cov}(z, y_a) = 0$$

so that

$$\gamma_i = \text{cov}(y_i, y_a)/\text{var}(y_a)$$

and we have the sterling pricing relation

$$q_i = \varepsilon E y_i - (q_a - \varepsilon E y_a)\text{cov}(y_i, y_a)/\text{var}(y_a).$$

Let b be a dollar risk-free portfolio. Then γ_b is zero so that

$$\text{cov}(y_b, y_a) = 0,$$

but

$$\text{var}(y_b) = \text{var}(\alpha_b z + \gamma_b y_a) = \alpha_b^2 \text{var}(z) > 0,$$

so that b is not a sterling risk-free portfolio. Applying the sterling pricing relation to b gives

$$q_b = \varepsilon E y_b,$$

so that

$$\varepsilon = q_b / E y_b$$

is the sterling discount factor for a portfolio whose payoff is uncorrelated with the market payoff.

This sterling pricing relation is a precise analogue of the dollar pricing relation

$$p_i = \delta E x_i - (p_a - \delta E x_a) \operatorname{cov}(x_i, x_a)/\operatorname{var}(x_a)$$

except that the discount factor is that for a portfolio whose payoff is uncorrelated with the market payoff, rather than the risk-free discount factor.

Thus although the specific CAPM pricing relation, in which the discount factor is the discount factor for a risk-free portfolio, applies only in the given units of value this general CAPM pricing relation, in which the discount factor is the discount factor for a portfolio whose payoff is uncorrelated with the market payoff, applies in any units of value provided that the relevant exchange rate and market payoff are independent.

THE SECURITY MARKET LINE

For the remainder of this chapter we consider only securities whose prices are positive, and assume that the market portfolio also has a positive price. Then the pricing relation may be expressed in terms of rates of return, the rate of return of security i being

$$r_i = x_i / p_i - 1.$$

The pricing relation for security i then becomes

$$(\delta E x_i - p_i)/p_i = \gamma_i(\delta E x_a - p_a)/p_i,$$

or equivalently

$$E x_i/p_i - 1/\delta = (p_a/p_i)\gamma_i(E x_a/p_a - 1/\delta),$$

so that

$$E r_i - \rho = \beta_i(E r_a - \rho)$$

where

$$\rho = 1/\delta - 1$$

is the risk-free interest rate and

$$\beta_i = (p_a/p_i)\gamma_i = (\text{cov}(x_i, x_a)/p_i p_a)/(\text{var}(x_a)/p_a^2)$$

$$= \text{cov}(x_i/p_i, x_a/p_a)/\text{var}(x_a/p_a) = \text{cov}(r_i, r_a),$$

which constant is known as the beta of security i.

Thus the excess return of a security, that is, its expected return minus the risk-free interest rate, is proportional to the beta of the security, the constant of proportionality being the excess return of the market portfolio. Equivalently, the excess return of a security is proportional to the risk of the security as measured by the covariance of its return with the market return (rather than by, for example, the standard deviation of the return of the security).

This relation between excess return and beta, which applies at any probabilities, is the central CAPM property. The graph of this relation, which is known as the security market line, is illustrated in Figure 3.1; this figure identifies a risk-free portfolio b, with a beta of zero, and the market portfolio a, with a beta of unity.

Although the security market line in Figure 3.1 is upward-sloping this property is not ensured by the absence of

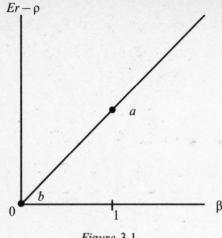

Figure 3.1

arbitrage: it applies if and only if the excess return of the market portfolio is positive.

Given any two (independent) securities the CAPM property determines the expected return of any other security. Consider the example in which the expected returns and betas of two securities, both of whose prices are unity, are given in Table 3.1.

Table 3.1

Security	Er	β
1	0.10	0.5
2	0.20	1.5

The CAPM property gives

$$0.10 - \rho = 0.5(Er_a - \rho)$$

$$0.20 - \rho = 1.5(Er_a - \rho).$$

Solving these two equations gives the risk-free interest rate ρ as 0.05 and the expected return of the market portfolio Er_a as 0.15. Then for any security i with a beta of β_i we have

$$Er_i = 0.05 + 0.10\beta_i.$$

THE CAPITAL MARKET LINE

Given some arbitrary probabilities a portfolio is mean-variance efficient if there is no portfolio with the same variance of return and a higher expected return.

Since security prices are positive a portfolio c may be represented by a list of weights w, where

$$w_i = p_i c_i / p.c$$

for each security i, such that

$$g(w) = \sum_i w_i = 1.$$

The return of this portfolio is

$$r_c = \sum_i w_i r_i$$

so that the expected return is

$$f(w) = Er_c = \sum_i w_i Er_i$$

and the variance of return is

$$h(w) = \text{var}(r_c) = \sum_i \sum_j w_i w_j \text{cov}(r_i, r_j).$$

Then a portfolio c whose (positive) variance of return is σ^2 is mean-variance efficient if the weights representing it maximise $f(w)$ subject to

$$g(w) = 1$$

and

$$h(w) = \sigma^2.$$

It follows from the Lagrangean theorem that this maximisation problem has a unique solution characterised by

$$\partial f(w)/\partial w_i - \lambda \partial g(w)/\partial w_i - \mu \partial h(w)/\partial w_i = 0$$

for each security i where λ and μ are constants. Thus at this maximum we have

$$\mathrm{E}r_i - \lambda = 2\mu \sum_j w_j \mathrm{cov}(r_i, r_j) = 2\mu \mathrm{cov}(r_i, \sum_j w_j r_j) = 2\mu \mathrm{cov}(r_i, r_c)$$

for each security (or portfolio) i.

Applying the maximum condition to some portfolio b whose return is uncorrelated with the return of c we have

$$\mathrm{E}r_b - \lambda = 0,$$

so that λ is the expected return of this portfolio. Applying the condition to the portfolio c we have

$$\mathrm{E}r_c - \lambda = 2\mu \mathrm{var}(r_c),$$

so that

$$2\mu = (\mathrm{E}r_c - \lambda)/\mathrm{var}(r_c).$$

It follows that the portfolio c is mean-variance efficient if and only if

$$\mathrm{E}r_i - \lambda = (\mathrm{E}r_c - \lambda)\,\mathrm{cov}(r_i, r_c)/\mathrm{var}(r_c)$$

for each security i where λ is the expected return of some portfolio whose return is uncorrelated with the return of c. This result does not depend on the assumption that security payoffs are linearly related to market payoffs, and is thus independent of the units of value in which payoffs are measured. (The equivalent condition expressed in terms of payoffs, which applies whether or not security prices are positive, is

$$\delta Ex_i - p_i = (\delta Ex_a - p_a)\operatorname{cov}(x_i, x_c)/\operatorname{var}(x_c)$$

where

$$\delta = p_b/Ex_b.)$$

Since the CAPM property is

$$Er_i - \rho = (Er_a - \rho)\operatorname{cov}(r_i, r_a)/\operatorname{var}(r_a)$$

for each security i where a is the market portfolio and ρ the expected return of some portfolio whose return is uncorrelated with the return of a it follows that the market portfolio a is mean-variance efficient. Conversely, if a is mean-variance efficient then

$$Er_i - \lambda = (Er_a - \lambda)\operatorname{cov}(r_i, r_a)/\operatorname{var}(r_a)$$

for each security i where λ is the expected return of some portfolio whose return is uncorrelated the return of a, which is the CAPM property. Thus the CAPM property is equivalent to the mean-variance efficiency of the market portfolio.

Since the returns of all risk-free portfolios, that is all portfolios with a variance of return of zero, are the same any risk-free portfolio is mean-variance efficient. Let d be a linear combination of a risk-free portfolio b and some mean-variance efficient portfolio c. Then

$$r_d = (1-\theta)\rho + \theta r_c$$

for some number θ, so that

$$Er_d - \rho = (1-\theta)\rho + \theta Er_c - \rho = \theta(Er_c - \rho),$$

$$\operatorname{cov}(r_i, r_d) = \operatorname{cov}(r_i, \theta r_c) = \theta\operatorname{cov}(r_i, r_c)$$

for each security i, and

$$\mathrm{var}(r_d) = \mathrm{var}(\theta r_c) = \theta^2 \mathrm{var}(r_c).$$

It follows that

$$\mathrm{E}r_i - \rho = (\mathrm{E}r_d - \rho)\,\mathrm{cov}(r_i, r_d)/\mathrm{var}(r_d)$$

for each security i. Since ρ is the (expected) return of a portfolio whose return is uncorrelated with the return of d it follows that d is mean-variance efficient. Thus any linear combination of a risk-free portfolio and a mean-variance efficient portfolio is mean-variance efficient.

Conversely, let d be a mean-variance efficient portfolio (with positive variance of return) and h be a linear combination of an arbitrary risk-free portfolio b and an arbitrary mean-variance efficient portfolio c such that the variance of return of h is the same as that of d. Then as h is a linear combination of b and c it is mean-variance efficient. Since the portfolio weights which maximise expected return for any given positive variance of return are unique the portfolio weights for d are the same as those for h, so that d is a multiple of h and thus a linear combination of b and c. Thus any mean-variance efficient portfolio is a linear combination of an arbitrary risk-free portfolio and an arbitrary mean-variance efficient portfolio .

This result is known as the two-fund separation theorem. Any mean-variance efficient portfolio may be constructed using two constituent funds: a risk-free portfolio and an arbitrary mean-variance efficient portfolio. Again, this result does not depend on the assumption that security payoffs are linearly related to market payoffs, provided that there exists some risk-free portfolio. However, if security payoffs are linearly related to market payoffs then any mean-variance efficient portfolio is a linear combination of a risk-free portfolio and the market portfolio.

Since any mean-variance efficient portfolio is a linear combination of an arbitrary risk-free portfolio and an arbitrary mean-variance efficient portfolio and since any linear combination of a risk-free portfolio and a mean-variance efficient portfolio is mean-variance efficient it follows that any linear combination of mean-variance efficient portfolios is mean-variance efficient.

Assume that d is a mean-variance efficient portfolio, say

$$d = \varepsilon b + \gamma c$$

where b is a risk-free portfolio and c is an arbitrary mean-variance efficient portfolio. Then the excess return of d is

$$E r_d - \rho = \theta (E r_c - \rho)$$

and the standard deviation of return is

$$\text{std}(r_d) = \sqrt{\text{var}(r_d)} = \theta \sqrt{\text{var}(r_c)} = \theta \, \text{std}(r_c),$$

where

$$\theta = \varepsilon / (\varepsilon + \gamma).$$

It follows that

$$E r_d - \rho = \text{std}(r_d) \, (E r_c - \rho) / \text{std}(r_c).$$

Thus the excess return of a mean-variance efficient portfolio is proportional to the portfolio's standard deviation of return σ, the constant of proportionality being the excess return of any mean-variance efficient portfolio per unit of its standard deviation of return. The graph of this relation, which is known as the capital market line, is illustrated in Figure 3.2; this figure identifies a risk-free portfolio b with a standard deviation of return of zero and the market portfolio a.

Although the capital market line in Figure 3.2 is upward-sloping this property is not ensured by the absence of arbitrage: it applies if and only if the excess return of the market portfolio is positive, that is, if and only if the security market line is upward-sloping.

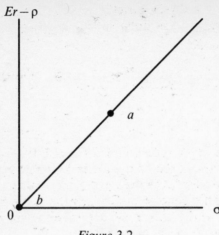

Figure 3.2

EVIDENCE

Tests of the CAPM, as of any expectational model, require that unobservable expectations be represented by observable outcomes: typically, by sample means. Tests of the CAPM, in particular, also require that the unobservable market portfolio be represented by some observable proxy: typically, by some market index.

Black, Jensen and Scholes (1972) represent expectations by sample means and the market portfolio by a market index (for the USA). Ten portfolios are constructed by estimating the covariance of the return of each security with the index return from a time-series sample and ranking securities according to these estimated covariances. The first portfolio consists of the securities in the first decile of estimated covariances, or equivalently of estimated betas, and so forth. The expected returns and betas of each of these portfolios are then estimated from a new time-series sample.

These expected returns Er_i and betas β_i for each portfolio i, expressed in dollar terms, are used to estimate the parameters λ and μ of the cross section equation

$$Er_i = \lambda + \mu\beta_i$$

using regression analysis. Strictly, this is a test of the specific CAPM, denominated in dollars. This model implies that

$$\lambda = \rho$$

and

$$\mu = Er_a - \rho,$$

where r_a is the index return and ρ the risk-free interest rate. However, it is also a test of the general CAPM provided that the relevant dollar exchange rate and index returns are independent. This general model has the same implications except that ρ is the return of a portfolio whose return is uncorrelated with the index return.

Evidence on the independence of dollar exchange rates and index returns is provided by Solnik's (1974) estimates of the correlations between the dollar exchange rates of various currencies and index returns (for the USA), which are given in Table 3.2.

Table 3.2

Currency	Correlation
Sterling	0.10
Yen	0.08
D-Mark	0.16
S-Franc	0.03

The correlation is low for each currency.

The means and *t*-statistics of the estimates of the parameters λ and μ, with returns expressed as annual percentages, together with the values implied by the specific and general models, are given in Table 3.3. Neither coefficient is approximately equal to its value as implied by the specific CAPM, but both coefficients are approximately equal to their values as implied by the general CAPM.

Table 3.3

	λ	μ
Mean	6.2	13.0
t-statistic	8.9	21.7
Specific	1.9	17.0
General	6.0	12.9

A similar approach is adopted by Fama and MacBeth (1973). The expected returns Er_i and betas β_i for each portfolio i, again expressed in dollar terms, are used to estimate the parameters λ, μ, ν and π of the equation

$$Er_i = \lambda + \mu\beta_i + \nu\beta_i^2 + \pi\sigma_i$$

where

$$\sigma_i = \sqrt{[\mathrm{var}(r_i) - \beta_i^2 \mathrm{var}(r_a)]},$$

r_a being the proxy return. The term involving β_i^2 is included to test for any non-linearity in the relation between excess return and beta, and the term involving σ_i to test for any influence of variance which is not explained by beta and the variance of index returns, noting that if

$$r_i = \alpha_i + \beta_i r_a$$

then

$$\mathrm{var}(r_i) = \beta_i^2 \mathrm{var}(r_a)$$

so that σ_i is zero.

The general model implies that ν and π are both zero and, since the excess return of the index portfolio is positive, that μ is positive. The specific model implies, in addition to these properties, that λ is equal to the risk-free interest rate.

The equation is estimated without restrictions, and also with ν restricted to zero, with π restricted to zero, and with both ν and π restricted to zero. The means and *t*-statistics of the estimates of the various parameters, with returns expressed as annual percentages, are given in Table 3.4.

Table 3.4

		λ	μ	ν	100π
Unrestricted	Mean	2.4	13.7	−3.1	5.2
	t-statistic	0.6	1.9	−0.9	1.1
$\nu = 0$	Mean	6.5	8.6		2.0
	t-statistic	2.1	2.1		0.5
$\pi = 0$	Mean	5.9	12.6	−1.0	
	t-statistic	1.9	1.8	−0.3	
$\nu = \pi = 0$	Mean	7.3	10.2		
	t-statistic	3.2	2.6		

The coefficient ν is not significantly different from zero whether π is restricted to zero or not, and the coefficient π is not significantly different from zero whether ν is restricted to zero or not. The coefficient μ is significantly positive, whether or not ν and π are restricted to zero. However, the coefficient λ is not approximately equal to the mean of the risk-free interest rate (which is 1.6).

A fundamental problem with the tests of Black, Jensen, and Scholes (1972) and of Fama and MacBeth (1973), and indeed of any tests of the CAPM, is that the market portfolio is unobservable and must thus be represented by a proxy.

Now the CAPM property is equivalent to the mean-variance efficiency of the market portfolio. Thus if the proxy portfolio is mean-variance efficient in some sample then the CAPM with respect to this proxy will hold precisely in that sample regardless of whether the market portfolio is mean-variance efficient, that is, regardless of whether the CAPM property holds with respect to the market portfolio. And conversely, if the proxy portfolio is not mean-variance efficient in some sample then the CAPM with respect to the proxy will not hold in the sample, regardless of whether it holds with respect to the market portfolio.

Assume that the following conditions apply: the CAPM holds approximately with respect to a proxy; proxy and market returns are highly correlated; and if the CAPM holds approximately with respect to a proxy *a* and the return of a portfolio *b* is highly correlated with the return of *a* then the CAPM holds approximately with respect to *b*. Then the acceptance of the CAPM with respect to a proxy portfolio would indicate the acceptance of the CAPM with respect to the market portfolio.

The first condition, at least for the general CAPM, is established by the tests discussed above. The second condition may be expected to apply if, as is the case, most individual returns are positively correlated and the market and proxy portfolios are both averages. The third condition, however, only applies weakly: for example, Roll (1977) shows that there is a portfolio with respect to which the specific CAPM holds precisely for the data of the Black, Jensen and Scholes (1972) test and whose correlation of return with the proxy used by Black, Jensen and Scholes is 0.9.

In the light of Roll's findings tests of the CAPM must be considered to be of low power.

FUND EVALUATION

The (specific) CAPM suggests that the performance of an investment fund may be measured by the difference between its actual return and its expected return conditional on the same risk as determined by the fund's beta and the return of the market portfolio. This gives the performance measure

$$\alpha_i = r_i - [\beta_i r_a + (1 - \beta)\rho]$$

where r_i is the fund return, r_a an index return, β_i the fund's beta and ρ the risk-free interest rate.

This approach is adopted by Jensen (1969), with the market portfolio represented by a market index. As a check on the validity of measuring the risk of a fund by its beta the mean betas of funds in each of five categories of investment objectives, and thus of perceived riskiness, are calculated. These means, with categories listed in decreasing order of perceived riskiness, are given in Table 3.5.

Table 3.5

Category	Beta
Growth	0.97
Growth-income	0.94
Income-growth	0.86
Income	0.67
Balanced	0.65

There is a negatively monotone relation between the perceived riskiness of a category and the mean beta of funds in that category.

The mean annual percentage performance measure is -0.9, indicating that the return of an average fund is lower than the return of an equal-beta portfolio consisting of a combination of a risk-free portfolio and the index portfolio. Indeed, the performance measures for some two-thirds of funds are negative. Since holding the equal-beta portfolio involves no administrative expenses a more appropriate measure may be one which excludes such expenses: if expenses are ignored the mean performance measure improves, but still remains negative.

Since this evaluation procedure necessarily uses a proxy for the market portfolio it suffers from the same problem as do tests of the CAPM. As Roll (1978) has shown, if the proxy portfolio is mean-variance efficient then the performance measure for each fund will be zero. On the other hand, if the proxy portfolio is not mean-variance efficient then individual performance measures will typically be non-zero, but whether the measure for a particular fund is positive or negative may depend on the proxy used.

In the light of this result the CAPM evaluation procedure, as the CAPM tests, must be considered to be of low power.

APPENDIX

The central CAPM property, that the excess return of a security is proportional to the covariance of its return with the return of a market index, may also be obtained as an equilibrium rather than an arbitrage relation.

In this framework the assumption that there is a meaningful (positive and risky) market portfolio is retained but the assumption that security payoffs are linearly related to market payoffs is replaced by four new assumptions: all agents assign the same probabilities to states; all agents evaluate portfolios solely on the basis of their expected returns and variances of returns (with a higher expectation being preferred to a lower for any given variance and a lower variance being preferred to a higher for any given expectation); there exist some equilibrium prices; and there exists some risk-free portfolio.

At these equilibrium prices, or equivalently rates of return, all agents' planned and actual portfolios are the same. Since each agent evaluates portfolios on the basis of their expected returns and variances of return, under some common probabilities, each agent's portfolio is mean-variance efficient, under these probabilities. Since, given the existence of a risk-free portfolio, the sum of mean-variance efficient portfolios is mean-variance efficient it follows that the aggregate portfolio, or equivalently the market portfolio, a, is mean-variance efficient. Then from the characterisation of mean-variance efficient portfolios

$$\mathrm{E}r_i - \rho = (\mathrm{E}r_a - \rho)\,\mathrm{cov}(r_i, r_a)/\mathrm{var}(r_a)$$

for each security i where ρ is the expected return of a portfolio b whose return is uncorrelated with the return of a, such as a risk-free portfolio. This is the equation of the security market line.

The first three assumptions employed in this framework are restrictive. First, agents may well differ in their probability assignments. Second, the evaluation of portfolios solely on the basis of their expected returns and variances of returns excludes other potentially relevant aspects. If an agent has some non-tradeable wealth, such as human capital, then the covariance of a portfolio's return with the return of this wealth may also be relevant. Even if agents have no such wealth the assessment of portfolios solely on this basis may be inappropriate. For example, assume that there are two states with probabilities of 0.9 and 0.1 respectively, and consider two portfolios c and d whose returns in each state are given by

$$r_c = (0.0,\ 1.0)$$

$$r_d = (0.2,\ -0.8);$$

each portfolio has an expected return of 0.10 and a variance of return 0.09, but portfolio c may well be preferred to portfolio d. And third, even if the two assumptions discussed above are satisfied no equilibrium may exist (see Allingham, 1991).

The assumption that there exists a risk-free portfolio is required only to obtain the specific CAPM. As is shown by Black (1972), the general CAPM may be obtained without this assumption.

BIBLIOGRAPHY

Allingham, M. (1991) 'Existence Theorems in the Capital Asset Pricing Model', *Econometrica*, no 59.

Black, F. (1972) 'Capital Market Equilibrium with Restricted Borrowing', *Journal of Business*, no. 45, pp. 444–55.

Black, F., Jensen, M. and Scholes, M. (1972) 'The Capital Asset Pricing Model: Some Empirical Tests', in M. Jensen (ed) *Studies in the Theory of Capital Markets* (New York: Praeger).

Brennan, M.J. (1989) 'Capital Asset Pricing Model', in J. Eatwell, M. Milgate and P. Newman (eds) *The New Palgrave: Finance* (London: Macmillan).

Fama, E. and MacBeth, J. (1973) 'Risk, Return and Equilibrium: Empirical Tests', *Journal of Political Economy*, no 81, pp. 607–36.

Jensen, M. (1969) 'Risk, the Pricing of Capital Assets, and the Evaluation of Investment Portfolios', *Journal of Business*, no 42, pp. 167–247.

Jensen, M. (1972) 'Capital Markets: Theory and Evidence', *Bell Journal of Economics and Management Science*, no 2, pp. 357–98.

Lancaster, K. (1968) *Mathematical Economics* (Toronto: Macmillan).

Lintner, J. (1965) 'The Valuation of Risk Assets and the Selection of Risky Investments in Stock Portfolios and Capital Budgets', *Review of Economics and Statistics*, no 47, pp. 13–37.

Roll, R. (1977) 'A Critique of the Asset Pricing Theory's Tests – Part 1: On Past and Potential Testability of the Theory', *Journal of Financial Economics*, no 4, pp. 129–76.

Roll, R. (1978) 'Ambiguity when Performance is Measured by the Security Market Line', *Journal of Finance*, no 33, pp. 1051–69.

Sharpe, W. (1964) 'Capital Asset Prices: A Theory of Market Equilibrium under Conditions of Risk', *Journal of Finance*, no 19, pp. 425–42.

Solnik, B. (1974) 'Stock Prices and Monetary Variables: The International Evidence', *Financial Analysts' Journal*, no 40, pp. 69–73.

4 Approximate Arbitrage: The Arbitrage Pricing Technique

This chapter extends the concept of arbitrage to encompass approximate arbitrage and develops the arbitrage pricing technique (or APT); this may be interpreted as a generalisation of the version of the CAPM developed in Chapter 3.

AN EXACT FACTOR MODEL

A factor is an aspect of the environment, such as the weather; it is specified by a value in each state, such as the inches of rainfall. Thus a factor is analogous to a security, or a portfolio, which is defined by its payoff in each state; the difference is that factors are not tradeable.

The exact factor model assumes that the payoffs of securities in some given units of value are linear functions of the values of a number k of factors. Then the payoff of security i is

$$x_i = \alpha_i + \sum_j \gamma_{ij} g_j$$

where α_i and

$$\gamma_{i1}, \ldots, \gamma_{ik}$$

are constants, representing the sensitivities of the payoff of security i to the values of the factors, and

$$g_1, \ldots, g_k$$

are the values of the k factors. It is assumed that the number k of factors is (substantially) less than the number n of securities, that the variance of the value of each factor is positive, and that factor values are linearly independent, in that none is a linear combination of the others. This restriction on the payoffs of securities is a weakening of the restriction involved in the CAPM. Indeed, the CAPM may be interpreted as an exact factor model with a single factor whose value is the payoff of a market portfolio.

Given some arbitrary probabilities the payoff of security i may be written as

$$x_i = \mathrm{E}x_i + \sum_j \gamma_{ij} f_j$$

where, for each factor j,

$$f_j = g_j - \mathrm{E}g_j$$

is a newly defined factor whose expected value is zero.

If the price p_i of security i is positive this relation may be written as

$$r_i = \mathrm{E}r_i + \sum_j \beta_{ij} f_j$$

where

$$r_i = x_i/p_i - 1$$

is the return of security i and, for each factor j,

$$\beta_{ij} = \gamma_{ij}/p_i$$

is the sensitivity of the return of security i to the value of factor j.

Choose some portfolio b such that

$$\alpha_b = \sum_i b_i \alpha_i > 0$$

and

$$\gamma_{bj} = \sum_i b_i \gamma_{ij} = 0$$

for each factor j. It follows from the solution theorem for homogeneous equations that such a choice is possible as it imposes only $k+1$ restrictions on the n portfolio quantities. Then

$$x_b = \alpha_b > 0$$

so that b is a risk-free portfolio.

Applying the martingale property we have

$$p_i = \delta \hat{E} x_i$$

for each security i where δ is the risk-free discount factor and $\hat{E}$ the martingale expectation operator. We then have the pricing relation

$$p_i = \delta E x_i + \sum_j \gamma_{ij} \delta \hat{E} f_j = \delta E x_i - \sum_j \gamma_{ij} \lambda_j$$

for each security (or portfolio) i where

$$\lambda_j = -\delta \hat{E} f_j$$

for each factor j.

This pricing relation gives the price of security i as its discounted expected payoff $E x_i$ minus a risk element associated with each factor, the element associated with factor j being the product of γ_{ij} and λ_j. The first term in this product, γ_{ij}, is the sensitivity of the payoff of x_i with respect to the value of factor j. Since $E f_j$ is zero the second term,

$$\lambda_j = -\delta \hat{E} f_j = \delta(E f_j - \hat{E} f_j),$$

may be interpreted as the risk premium associated with factor j, that is the discounted difference between the expected value of the factor at the arbitrary probabilities and that at the martingale probabilities. Thus the risk element for security i associated with factor j is the product of the security's sensitivity with respect to the factor and the risk premium associated with the factor.

If p_i is positive we may write the pricing relation for the security as

$$\mathrm{E}r_i - \rho = \sum_j \beta_{ij} \mu_j$$

where

$$\rho = 1/\delta - 1$$

is the risk-free interest rate and, for each factor j,

$$\mu_j = \lambda_j / \delta$$

is the terminal value of the risk premium associated with the factor.

Thus the excess return of a security is a linear combination of its factor sensitivities, the weight attached to each sensitivity being the terminal value of the risk premium associated with the corresponding factor. This relation between excess return and the k factor sensitivities, which applies at any probabilities, is the APT property; its graph is known as the security market plane.

Given any $k + 1$ (independent) securities the APT property determines the expected return of any other security. Consider the example with two factors in which the expected returns and factor sensitivities of three securities, all of whose prices are unity, are given in Table 4.1.

Table 4.1

Security	Er	β_1	β_2
1	0.240	1.0	1.0
2	0.248	1.6	0.6
3	0.250	0.5	1.5

The APT property gives

$$0.240 - \rho = 1.0\mu_1 + 1.0\mu_2$$

$$0.248 - \rho = 1.6\mu_1 + 0.6\mu_2$$

$$0.250 - \rho = 0.5\mu_1 + 1.5\mu_2.$$

Solving these three equations gives the risk-free rate of interest ρ as 0.06 and the terminal values of the risk premiums μ_1 and μ_2 associated with the two factors as 0.08 and 0.10 respectively. Then for any security i with the factor sensitivities β_{i1} and β_{i2} we have

$$r_i = 0.06 + 0.08\beta_{i1} + 0.10\beta_{i2}.$$

MEAN-VARIANCE EFFICIENCY

Mean-variance efficiency is best investigated by redefining factors so that they are symmetric. This is achieved by choosing k new factors, each of which has an expected value of zero and a variance of unity, such that the covariance between the values of factors j and h is zero for each j and h. Such a choice is possible as it imposes only $k+2$ homogeneous restrictions on the m values of each factor. Since these factors are uncorrelated they are linearly independent.

It follows from the basis theorem (see Lancaster, 1968; R2.3) that if all vectors in some set are linear combinations of some k linearly independent vectors then they are linear combinations of any k linearly independent vectors. Thus we may write the payoff of security i minus its expectation as a linear combination of the new factors, that is, write

$$x_i - \mathrm{E}x_i = \sum_j \gamma_{ij} f_j$$

where (in the interest of notational simplicity) f_j is now the vector of values of the new factor j and γ_{ij} the sensitivity of the payoff of security i with respect to this new factor. Since the new factors are uncorrelated

$$\text{cov}(x_i, f_j) = \text{cov}(\gamma_{ij}f_j, f_j) = \gamma_{ij}\text{var}(f_j) = \gamma_{ij}.$$

Consider factor 1, say, and choose some portfolio d such that

$$\text{E}x_d = \sum_i d_i \text{E}x_i = 0,$$

$$\gamma_{d1} = \sum_i d_i \gamma_{i1} = 1$$

and

$$\gamma_{dj} = \sum_i d_i \gamma_{ij} = 0$$

for each factor j other than factor 1. The payoff of this portfolio is

$$x_d = \text{E}x_d + \sum_j \gamma_{ij} f_j = f_1,$$

so that the portfolio d replicates factor 1. The price of this replicating portfolio is

$$p_d = \delta \text{E}x_d - \sum_j \gamma_{dj}\lambda_j = -\lambda_1.$$

Let c be a (positive) value-weighted average of the k replicating portfolios, that is, let

$$c_j = \theta p_j > 0$$

for each replicating portfolio j, where

$$\theta = 1 / \sum_j p_j < 0.$$

The payoff of portfolio c is

$$x_c = \sum_j c_j f_j$$

so that for any security (or portfolio) i

$$\text{cov}(x_i, x_c) = \sum_j c_j \text{cov}(x_i, f_j)$$

$$= \theta \sum_j p_j \gamma_{ij}$$

$$= -\theta \sum_j \gamma_{ij} \lambda_j$$

$$= -\theta(\delta E x_i - p_i).$$

Applying this result to the portfolio c we have

$$\text{var}(x_c) = -\theta(\delta E x_c - p_c)$$

so that

$$\delta E x_i - p_i = (\delta E x_c - p_c) \text{cov}(x_i, x_c)/\text{var}(x_c)$$

for each security i.

This statement is the condition for the portfolio c to be mean-variance efficient. Since any mean-variance efficient portfolio may be constructed from a risk-free portfolio and an arbitrary mean-variance efficient portfolio it follows that any mean-variance efficient portfolio may be constructed from a risk-free portfolio and a value-weighted (or equivalently a risk premium-weighted) average of the k portfolios which respectively replicate the k new factors.

AN APPROXIMATE FACTOR MODEL

The approximate factor model assumes that the payoff of a security in some given units of value is a linear function of the values of k factors, each representing a systematic risk, and an unsystematic risk component which is idiosyncratic to the security. Then given some probabilities the payoff of security i is

$$x_i = E x_i + \sum_j \gamma_{ij} f_j + u_i$$

where u_i is the idiosyncratic risk component for security i.

Since the expected value of each factor is zero

$$\mathrm{E}u_i = -\sum_j \gamma_{ij} f_j = 0$$

for each security i, so that the expected value of each idiosyncratic risk component is zero. It is assumed that

$$\mathrm{cov}(u_i, f_j) = 0$$

for each security i and factor j, and that

$$\mathrm{cov}(u_i, u_h) = 0$$

for each pair of securities i and h.

An important property of the assumptions concerning the idiosyncratic risk components is that, in contrast to the assumptions of the exact factor model (or of the CAPM), they place restrictions on the probabilities associated with states as well as on the payoffs of the various securities in these states. This means that the analysis will apply only for probabilities which satisfy these restrictions rather than for arbitrary probabilities.

A further property of the assumptions on the idiosyncratic risk components is that, again in contrast to the assumptions of the exact factor model (or of the CAPM), the payoff relation does not in general apply to portfolios. For example, if

$$a = (1, 1)$$

then

$$x_a = \mathrm{E}x_a + \sum_j \gamma_{aj} f_j + u_a$$

and

$$\mathrm{cov}(u_a, f_j) = \mathrm{cov}(u_1, f_j) + \mathrm{cov}(u_2, f_j) = 0$$

as required, but

$$\mathrm{cov}(u_a, u_1) = \mathrm{cov}(u_1, u_1) + \mathrm{cov}(u_2, u_1) = \mathrm{var}(u_1).$$

As in general the variance of u_i is positive this violates the assumptions. Thus the analysis must exclude securities which are (effectively) portfolios.

Applying the martingale property to the approximate factor model we have the pricing relation

$$p_i = \delta E x_i - \sum_j \gamma_{ij} \lambda_j - \mu_i$$

where

$$\mu_i = -\delta \hat{E} u_i = \delta (E u_i - \hat{E} u_i)$$

may be interpreted as the risk element associated with u_i, or the idiosyncratic risk premium for security i.

The idiosyncratic risk premium for a well-diversified portfolio a is the risk premium associated with the sum of many uncorrelated individual idiosyncratic risk components. Since this sum may be expected to be small the corresponding risk premium may also be expected to be small. That is, idiosyncratic risk may be reduced by diversification.

For example, if the absolute value of each security holding a_i is the same, that is $1/n$, then

$$\text{var}(u_a) = \text{var}\left(\sum_i u_i/n\right) = \sum_i \text{var}(u_i)/n^2 = \sigma^2/n$$

where

$$\sigma^2 = \sum_i \text{var}(u_i)/n$$

is the average variance of the idiosyncratic risk components. Then if n is sufficiently large the variance of u_a is approximately zero, so that u_a is approximately constant. In this case

$$E u_a \approx \hat{E} u_a$$

so that

$$\mu_a = \delta (E u_a - \hat{E} u_a) \approx 0.$$

Since on average individual idiosyncratic risk premiums are small the price of security i is given by the approximation

$$p_i \approx \delta \mathrm{E} x_i - \sum_j \gamma_{ij} \lambda_j.$$

Equivalently, the excess return of a security i whose price is positive is given by the approximation

$$\mathrm{E} r_i - \rho \approx \sum_j \beta_{ij} \mu_j.$$

Thus the APT property holds approximately, in that the excess return of a security is an approximate linear combination of its factor sensitivities, the weight attached to each sensitivity being the terminal value of the risk premium associated with the corresponding factor.

UNITS OF VALUE

Assume that the payoff relations

$$x_i = \mathrm{E} x_i + \sum_j \gamma_{ij} f_j + u_i$$

apply when payoffs are denominated in dollars and let z be the sterling–dollar, say, exchange rate. Then

$$y_i = (\mathrm{E} x_i) z + \sum_j \gamma_{ij} h_j + v_i$$

for each security i where y_i and v_i are the sterling payoff of and idiosyncratic risk component for security i and, for each j, h_j is a a new factor. This relation may be written as

$$y_i = (\mathrm{E} y_i / \mathrm{E} z) z + \sum_j \gamma_{ij} [h_j - (\mathrm{E} h_j / \mathrm{E} z) z] + [v_i - (\mathrm{E} v_i / \mathrm{E} z) z],$$

noting that the exchange rate, and thus $\mathrm{E} z$, is positive.

Apart from the constant term this relation may be interpreted as an approximate factor model payoff relation for y_i in which the value of the new factor j is

$$h_j - (\mathrm{E} h_j / \mathrm{E} z) z$$

for each j and the value of the new idiosyncratic risk component is

$$v_i - (Ev_i/Ez)z.$$

In general, however, these new factors will each be correlated with the new idiosyncratic risk component because of the common influence of the exchange rate z. For the same reason, the new idiosyncratic risk components of different securities will also be correlated. Thus the assumptions concerning idiosyncratic risk components will not be satisfied and diversification will not ensure that the idiosyncratic risk component is small, and thus that the APT property holds approximately.

Now assume that the exchange rate and each sterling idiosyncratic risk component v_i, or equivalently the exchange rate and each dollar idiosyncratic risk component u_i, are independent. Then as Eu_i is zero Ev_i is also zero, so that

$$v_i - (Ev_i/Ez)z = v_i.$$

Also, as

$$Eu_i u_h = 0$$

for each pair of securities i and h

$$Ev_i v_h = 0,$$

so that the new idiosyncratic risk components are uncorrelated.

Similarly, if we assume that the exchange rate and each sterling factor h_j, or equivalently the exchange rate and each dollar factor f_j, are independent then

$$h_j - (Eh_j/Ez)z = h_j$$

and

$$Eh_j v_i = 0$$

for each security i so that the new factors and idiosyncratic risk components are uncorrelated.

Under these independence assumptions we may write the sterling payoff relation for security i as

$$y_i = (Ey_i/Ez)z + \sum_j \gamma_{ij}h_j + v_i$$

where v_i and h_j are uncorrelated for each factor j, and v_i and v_h are uncorrelated for each security h other than i. Applying the martingale property we have the sterling pricing relation

$$q_i = \varepsilon Ey_i - \sum_j \gamma_{ij}v_j - \theta_i$$

for each security i where q_i is the sterling price,

$$v_j = \delta(Eh_j - \hat{E}h_j)$$

is the risk premium associated with factor j,

$$\theta_i = \delta(Ev_i - \hat{E}v_i)$$

is the idiosyncratic risk premium, and

$$\varepsilon = \delta\hat{E}z/Ez$$

is the dollar discount rate multiplied by the currency risk factor.

Since idiosyncratic risk premiums are small on average the sterling price of security i is given by the approximation

$$q_i \approx \varepsilon Ey_i - \sum_j \gamma_{ij}v_j.$$

Applying this relation to a portfolio whose payoff is uncorrelated with each factor, that is a portfolio b for which γ_{bj} is zero for each factor j, we have

$$q_b \approx \varepsilon Ey_b$$

so that, approximately, ε is the discount factor for a portfolio with only idiosyncratic risk.

This approximate sterling pricing relation is a precise analogue of the approximate dollar pricing relation

$$p_i \approx \delta \mathrm{E} x_i - \sum_j \gamma_{ij} \lambda_j$$

except that the discount factor is (approximately) that for a portfolio with only idiosyncratic risk rather than the risk-free discount factor.

Thus the APT property holds approximately in any units of value, with the appropriate modification to the discount rate, provided that the relevant exchange rate and the values of each factor, and this exchange rate and each idiosyncratic risk component, are independent.

INFINITE MARKETS

The approximate nature of the APT property may be expressed more precisely when there are many securities. We thus extend the discussion to a (countably) infinite number of (independent) securities; this requires that there is an infinite number of states.

An approximate arbitrage opportunity exists if there is a (finite) costless portfolio which has an arbitrarily large expected payoff and an arbitrarily small payoff variance. That is, an approximate arbitrage opportunity exists if, given any (large) expected payoff μ and any (small) positive payoff variance σ^2 there is some finite portfolio a such that

$$p.a = 0,$$

$$\mathrm{E} x_a > \mu$$

and

$$\mathrm{var}(x_a) < \sigma^2,$$

where p is now a list of the prices of the securities comprising the finite portfolio a.

Given some arbitrary probabilities, now defined over the infinite number of states, we continue to assume the payoff relation

$$x_i = \mathrm{E}x_i + \sum_j \gamma_{ij} f_j + u_i$$

for each security i where u_i and f_j are uncorrelated for each factor j and u_i and u_h are uncorrelated for each security h other than i. We also assume that the variances of the idiosyncratic risk components are bounded, that is that there is some constant α such that

$$\mathrm{var}(u_i) < \alpha$$

for each security i.

For some integer n consider a set of n securities and choose the constants

$$\delta, \lambda_1, \ldots, \lambda_k, c_1, \ldots, c_n$$

to satisfy the equations

$$\sum_i p_i c_i = 0,$$

$$\sum_i c_i \gamma_{ij} = 0$$

for each of the k factors j, and

$$c_i = \delta \mathrm{E}x_i - \sum_j \gamma_{ij} \lambda_j - p_i$$

for each of the n securities i. It follows from the solution theorem for non-homogeneous equations (see Lancaster, 1968; R3.4) that such a choice is possible as there are $n+k+1$ equations and $n+k+1$ constants.

Let

$$\theta = (c.c)^{-3/4}$$

and consider the portfolio

$$a = \theta c,$$

the cost of which is

$$p.a = \theta \sum_i p_i c_i = 0.$$

Since

$$\gamma_{cj} = \sum_i c_i \gamma_{ij} = 0$$

for each factor j,

$$\delta E x_c = \sum_i c_i \delta E x_i = \sum_i c_i^2 + \sum_j (\sum_i c_i \gamma_{ij}) \lambda_j + \sum_i c_i p_i$$

$$= \sum_i c_i^2 = c.c$$

and

$$u_c = \sum_i c_i u_i = c.u.$$

It follows that

$$x_c = E x_c + \sum_j (\sum_i c_i \gamma_{ij}) f_j + c.u = (1/\delta) c.c + c.u$$

so that

$$x_a = (\theta/\delta) c.c + \theta c.u.$$

Then

$$E x_a = (\theta/\delta) c.c = (1/\delta)(c.c)^{1/4}$$

and

$$\operatorname{var}(x_a) = \operatorname{var}(\theta c.u) = \theta^2 \sum_i c_i^2 \operatorname{var}(u_i)$$

$$< \theta^2 \sum_i c_i^2 \alpha = \alpha \theta^2 c.c = \alpha (c.c)^{-1/2}.$$

Suppose that we may choose increasing sets of securities in such a way that $c.c$ becomes arbitrarily large as the number of securities n increases. Then

$$Ex_a = (1/\delta)(c.c)^{1/4}$$

becomes arbitrarily large and

$$\text{var}(x_a) < \alpha(c.c)^{-1/2}$$

becomes arbitrarily close to zero, as n increases. Thus given any μ and positive σ^2 there is some sufficiently large value of n for which

$$Ex_a > \mu$$

and

$$\text{var}(x_a) < \sigma^2.$$

Since $p.a$ is zero for all values of n this constitutes an approximate arbitrage opportunity.

It follows that in the absence of an approximate arbitrage opportunity $c.c$ does not become arbitrarily large as n increases, that is, there is some constant ε such that

$$c.c < \varepsilon$$

for all values of n; equivalently, for sufficiently large values of n

$$c.c/n < \varepsilon/n$$

becomes arbitrarily close to zero.

Since

$$c.c/n = \sum_i (\delta E x_i - \sum_j \gamma_{ij}\lambda_j - p_i)^2/n$$

this implies that the mean squared difference between

$$\delta E x_i - \sum_j \gamma_{ij} \lambda_j$$

and p_i becomes arbitrarily small as the number of securities increases, so that the approximation

$$p_i \approx \delta E x_i - \sum_j \gamma_{ij} \lambda_j$$

holds almost exactly, on average, in sufficiently large markets.

EVIDENCE

Tests of the APT, as tests of the CAPM, require that unobservable expectations be represented by sample means. However, in contrast to tests of the CAPM, which require that the 'market portfolio factor' be represented by some proxy, tests of the APT may either infer the values of factors by statistical methods or specify these independently.

The approach which infers the values of factors by statistical methods is adopted by Roll and Ross (1980). Securities are assembled into arbitrary groups, and in each group the number of factors and their sensitivities are estimated from a time series sample using the statistical technique of factor analysis (see Morrison, 1967; 8.3, 8.4).

Factor analysis estimates, for any integer k, the probability that no more than k factors are required to explain security returns. On the basis of these probabilities the number of factors is taken to be five: in more than a third of the groups the probability that five factors is sufficient exceeds 0.9, and in more than three-quarters of the groups this probability exceeds 0.5.

The five sensitivities β_{ij} obtained by factor analysis together with the expected returns $E r_i$ for each security i in the group are used to estimate the parameters

$$\mu, \lambda_1, \ldots, \lambda_5$$

of the cross-section equation

$$E r_i = \mu + \sum_j \lambda_j \beta_{ij}$$

using generalised least squares regression analysis (see Johnston, 1984; 8.3).

The coefficient μ, which represents the interest rate, may either be determined endogenously by considering there to be a constant sixth factor, or may be specified exogenously as the risk-free rate.

Since factor analysis determines sensitivities only up to a multiple it is the statistical significance of the risk premium coefficients rather than their numerical values which is material. The proportion of groups with at least k significant risk premium coefficients, for each value of k from 1 to 5, are given in Table 4.2. Proportions are given for the exogenous case in which the constant coefficient is specified exogenously as 6 (as an annual percentage), for the endogenous case in which the constant coefficient is determined endogenously, and, as a standard of comparison, for the chance case in which the true value of each risk premium coefficient is zero.

Table 4.2

	1 factor	2 factors	3 factors	4 factors	5 factors
Exogenous	0.88	0.57	0.33	0.17	0.05
Endogenous	0.69	0.48	0.07	0.05	0.00
Chance	0.23	0.02	0.00	0.00	0.00

Risk premium coefficients are more significant if the constant coefficient is specified exogenously. But whether this coefficient is exogenous or endogenous at least four factors' risk premiums are significant, with probabilities substantially in excess of those generated by chance alone. A fifth factor's risk premium is of marginal significance.

The APT may be tested against the alternative hypothesis that the volatility of a security's return, as measured by its standard deviation of return, influences expected return by estimating the coefficients

$$\mu, \lambda_1, \ldots, \lambda_5, \nu$$

of the cross-section equations

$$Er_i = \mu + \sum_j \lambda_j \beta_{ij} + \nu\sigma_i$$

for each security i, where σ_i is the standard deviation of return of the security.

The average t-statistic for the volatility coefficient, and the proportion of groups in which this coefficient is significant, are given in Table 4.3; also given are the corresponding average and proportion for the coefficient of the most significant sensitivity.

Table 4.3

	Average t-*statistic*	*Proportion*
Volatility	0.9	0.21
Sensitivity	2.3	0.57

The effect of volatility on expected return is insignificant, both absolutely and relative to the effect of the most significant sensitivity.

The alternative approach to testing the APT, which specifies the values of factors independently, is adopted by Chen, Roll and Ross (1986).

Since the payoff of a security may be considered to be the discounted value of its predicted future payoffs the applicable factors will be those which determine the relevant discount rate and payoffs. The discount rate may be interpreted as the sum of an average risk-free rate and a risk premium. The former is represented by the term structure, that is the difference between long- and short-term interest rates, and the latter by the difference between (long-term) risk-free and risky rates. Payoffs, at least for the equities considered, have real and monetary components. The former are represented by the rate of growth of real production, and the latter by both unanticipated inflation, that is the difference between actual and expected inflation, and by the change of expected inflation (expected inflation being measured by the difference between nominal and real interest rates).

Thus the five factors specified are the term structure (T), risk premium (R), production growth (P), unanticipated inflation (U) and expected inflation change (E). The correlations between each of these, and, for comparison, the return of a market index (I), are given in Table 4.4.

Table 4.4

	T	R	P	U	E
R	−0.75				
P	−0.16	0.22			
U	−0.10	0.18	−0.07		
E	−0.39	0.27	0.06	0.38	
I	0.25	0.04	0.02	−0.11	0.12

With the exception of the factors T and R, both of which involve the long-term risk-free rate, correlations between the five factors are low. Thus the factors have sufficient independence to generate a diverse pattern of returns.

Twenty portfolios are constructed by grouping securities according to their open interest. For each portfolio i the expected return Er_i, the sensitivities β_{ij} for each factor j, and the sensitivity σ_i of return with respect to the index I are estimated using time-series regression analysis.

These expected returns and sensitivities are then used to estimate the parameters

$$\mu, \lambda_1, \ldots, \lambda_5, \nu$$

of the cross-section equation

$$Er_i = \mu + \sum_j \lambda_j \beta_{ij} + \nu \sigma_i.$$

These parameters are estimated both with ν restricted to zero, as a simple test of the APT, and with ν unrestricted, as a test of the APT against the alternative of the CAPM.

The means and t-statistics of the coefficients of the five factors and of the index, with returns expressed as annual percentages, are given in Table 4.5.

Table 4.5

		T	R	G	U	E	I
Restricted	Mean	−6.2	8.6	16.3	−0.8	−0.2	
	t-statistic	−1.7	2.6	3.6	−2.0	−1.6	
Unrestricted	Mean	−7.1	9.9	14.1	−1.0	−0.1	2.9
	t-statistic	−1.9	3.0	3.1	−2.4	−1.6	0.6

The coefficient of each factor, that is the risk element associated with the factor, is significant, though those for the factors T and E are only marginally so; this applies whether or not the index is included. However, the coefficient of the index itself is insignificant.

The insignificance of the market index contrasts with its significance in time-series estimates, where it is the most significant variable. Thus although the index appears to explain much of time-series movements in returns its sensitivity, or beta, fails to explain cross-section differences in return if account is taken of the appropriate factor sensitivities. The apparent explanatory power of the market index in tests of the CAPM using large portfolios may then only reflect the positive correlation between all large (positive) portfolios, including the index.

PORTFOLIO SELECTION

Portfolio selection using the CAPM is straightforward since risk is one-dimensional, being measured solely by beta. A mean-variance efficient portfolio is obtained as a linear combination of a risk-free portfolio and the market index portfolio, that is by indexation of the risky component of the portfolio. Further, any two agents with the same probability views and attitudes to risk will hold the same portfolios.

Portfolio selection under the APT is more complex since risk is multi-dimensional. A mean-variance efficient portfolio is not in general obtained by indexation, and agents with the same probability views and attitudes to (dollar) risk may not hold the same portfolios.

Consider the example where there are two factors, f_1 and f_2, which have unit variance and are uncorrelated. The terminal values of the risk premiums associated with the two factors, μ_1 and μ_2, are each unity. It is assumed that all portfolios considered are sufficiently diversified as to have no idiosyncratic risk.

Let b be a risk-free portfolio, so that β_{bj} is zero for each factor j, and c be a risk premium-weighted average of portfolios replicating the two factors, so that

$$\beta_{cj} = \mu_j = 1$$

for each factor j. Then any linear combination of b and c is a mean-variance efficient portfolio.

Since the sensitivity with respect to some factor of a linear combination of portfolios is a linear combination of the sensitivities of each portfolio the set of mean-variance efficient portfolios may be represented in the space of factor sensitivities (β_1, β_2) by a line passing through the points representing the portfolios b and c. Such a line is illustrated in Figure 4.1.

In general, the (arbitrary) market portfolio will not lie on this line. Assume, for example, that the market portfolio a has a sensitivity of 0.5 with respect to the first factor and 1.5 with respect to the second, as is the case in Figure 4.1. Then the excess return of the market portfolio is

$$\mathrm{E}r_a - \rho = 0.5\mu_1 + 1.5\mu_2 = 2.0$$

and the variance of return is

$$\mathrm{var}(r_a) = 0.5^2 \mathrm{var}(f_1) + 1.5^2 \mathrm{var}(f_2) = 2.5.$$

If d is a portfolio with the same expected return as the market portfolio then

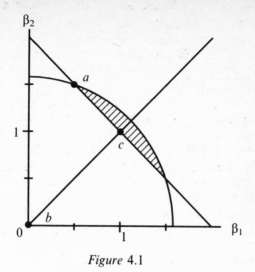

Figure 4.1

$$\mathrm{E} r_d - \rho = \beta_{d1}\mu_1 + \beta_{d2}\mu_2 = 2.0.$$

The set of such portfolios is represented by the line through *a* and *c*. Similarly, if *d* has the same variance of return as *a* then

$$\mathrm{var}(r_a) = \beta_{d1}^{\,2}\,\mathrm{var}(f_1) + \beta_{d2}^{\,2}\,\mathrm{var}(f_2) = 2.5.$$

The set of such portfolios is represented by the arc.

The shaded region represents the set of portfolios which are mean-variance superior to the market portfolio, in that they have both a higher expected return and a lower variance of return. The existence of such a region indicates that indexation is mean-variance inefficient.

Now assume that the first factor is identified with (unanticipated rises in) inflation and the second with (unanticipated falls in) interest rates, and consider two agents with the same probability views and attitudes to (dollar) risk.

The objective of the first agent, a pension fund, is to provide a secure standard of living for its beneficiaries. Accordingly, the agent will be particularly concerned with inflation and will thus hold a portfolio with a relatively large sensitivity to inflation. Then if inflation is high, and thus the needs of the beneficiaries are high, its income will be correspondingly high.

The objective of the second agent, a museum endowment, is to provide for the purchase of paintings; it is assumed that the prices of paintings are negatively correlated with interest rates. This agent will be particularly concerned with interest rates and will thus hold a portfolio with a relatively large sensitivity to interest rates. Then if interest rates are low, and thus the prices of paintings are high, its income will be correspondingly high.

In the space of factor sensitivities illustrated in Figure 4.1 the first agent will hold a portfolio below the line representing the set of mean-variance efficient portfolios and the second agent will hold a portfolio above this line. Thus agents with the same probability views and attitudes to (dollar) risk may hold different portfolios.

APPENDIX

The approximate APT property may alternatively be obtained as an equilibrium rather than an arbitrage relation. This equilibrium relation places an explicit bound on the divergence from linear pricing. This strengthening is achieved at the cost of additional assumptions though, in contrast to the equilibrium version of the CAPM, the assumption of a linear payoff relation is retained.

Given some arbitrary probabilities the linear payoff assumption is

$$x_i = \mathrm{E}x_i + \sum_j \gamma_{ij} f_j + u_i$$

for each security i where

$$\mathrm{cov}(u_i, f_j) = 0$$

for each factor j and

$$\text{cov}(u_i, u_h) = 0$$

for each security h other than i.

Consider factor 1, say, and choose some portfolio d such that

$$p_d = \sum_i d_i p_i = 0,$$

$$\gamma_{d1} = \sum_i d_i \gamma_{i1} = 1$$

and

$$\gamma_{dj} = \sum_i d_i \gamma_{ij} = 0$$

for each factor j other than 1. The payoff of this portfolio is

$$x_d = \text{E}x_d + f_1 + u_d.$$

The first additional assumption is that, through diversification, the portfolio d may be chosen so that u_d is zero. Then

$$x_d = \text{E}x_d + f_1 = (\delta \text{E}x_d - p_d)/\delta + f_1 = \lambda_1/\delta + f_1,$$

where

$$\lambda_1 = \delta \text{E}x_d - p_d$$

is the risk element associated with the portfolio d, or equivalently with factor 1. Such a portfolio is a basis portfolio for factor 1.

The remaining additional assumptions are those required in the equilibrium version of the CAPM: there exists a meaningful (positive) market portfolio; there exists some risk-free portfolio; all agents assign the same probabilities to states; all agents evaluate portfolios solely on the basis of their expected returns and variances of returns; and there exist some equilibrium prices.

Let b be a (risk-free) portfolio with unit payoff, and thus with a price of δ, the risk-free discount rate. Then for security i let a be a portfolio consisting of 1 unit of security i, $-p_i/\delta$

units of the risk-free portfolio b, and, for each factor j, $-\gamma_{ij}$ units of the basis portfolio for factor j. The price of this portfolio is

$$p_a = p_i - (p_i/\delta)\delta = 0$$

and its payoff is

$$x_a = x_i - p_i/\delta - \sum_j \gamma_{ij}(\lambda_j/\delta + f_j)$$

$$= \mathrm{E}x_i - p_i/\delta - \sum_j \gamma_{ij}\lambda_j/\delta + u_i.$$

Then the expected payoff is

$$\mathrm{E}x_a = \mathrm{E}x_i - p_i/\delta - \sum_j \gamma_{ij}\lambda_j/\delta,$$

so that

$$\delta\mathrm{E}x_a = \delta\mathrm{E}x_i - \sum_j \gamma_{ij}\lambda_j - p_i = \varepsilon$$

is the divergence from the linear pricing relation for security i.

Since each agent evaluates portfolios on the basis of their expected returns and variances of returns, under some common probabilities, each agent's portfolio is mean-variance efficient, under these probabilities. Consider an agent holding the mean-variance efficient portfolio c. Then there is no portfolio with the same variance of payoff as c and higher expected return, so that, in particular, the value of θ which maximises

$$g(\theta) = \mathrm{E}(x_c + \theta x_a)$$

subject to

$$h(\theta) = \mathrm{var}(x_c + \theta x_a) = \mathrm{var}(x_c) + \theta\mathrm{cov}(x_c, x_a) + \theta^2\mathrm{var}(x_a)$$

is zero.

It follows from the Lagrangean theorem that this maximising value of θ is given by

$$\partial g(\theta)/\partial\theta = \mu\partial h(\theta)/\partial\theta$$

where μ is a constant. As c is mean-variance efficient the addition of a portfolio θa to c which increases its expected return must also increase its variance of return, so that μ must be positive.

We thus have

$$\mathrm{E}x_a = \mu[\mathrm{cov}(x_c, x_a) + 2\theta\mathrm{var}(x_a)].$$

Setting θ equal to its solution value of zero gives

$$\mathrm{E}x_a = \mu\mathrm{cov}(x_c, x_a) = \mu\mathrm{cov}(\textstyle\sum_j\gamma_{cj}f_j + u_c, u_i)$$

$$= \mu[\textstyle\sum_j\gamma_{cj}\mathrm{cov}(f_j, u_i) + \mathrm{cov}(u_c, u_i)] = \mu\mathrm{cov}(u_c, u_i)$$

$$= \mu\mathrm{cov}(\textstyle\sum_h c_h u_h, u_i) = \mu c_i\,\mathrm{var}(u_i).$$

It follows that

$$\varepsilon_i = \delta\mathrm{E}x_a = \delta\mu c_i\,\mathrm{var}(u_i).$$

Since $\delta\mathrm{E}x_a$, δ, and $\mathrm{var}(u_i)$ are the same for each agent μc_i must also be the same for each agent. Further, since μ is positive for each agent, and market or aggregate security holdings are positive, c_i must be positive for each agent. As δ and $\mathrm{var}(u_i)$ are also positive it follows that ε_i is positive, so that

$$p_i < \delta\mathrm{E}x_i - \textstyle\sum_j\gamma_{ij}\lambda_j$$

and the linear pricing relation consistently over-predicts.

If p_i is positive then

$$\varepsilon_i/\delta p_i = \mathrm{E}x_i/p_i - \textstyle\sum_j(\gamma_{ij}/p_i)\lambda_j/\delta - 1/\delta = \mathrm{E}r_i - \rho - \textstyle\sum_j\beta_{ij}\mu_j > 0$$

is the divergence from the linear return relation for security i, and the linear return relation consistently under-predicts.

This divergence of return is given by

$$\varepsilon_i/\delta p_i = \mu c_i \mathrm{var}(u_i)/p_i = \mu p_i c_i \mathrm{var}(u_i/p_i) = \mu w(p_i c_i/w)\mathrm{var}(u_i/p_i)$$

where w is the agent's wealth. The product μw is known as the Rubinstein measure of relative risk aversion (see Rubinstein, 1973), $p_i c_i/w$ is the proportion of wealth held in security i, and $\mathrm{var}(u_i/p_i)$ is the variance of the idiosyncratic return of the security. In this case $\mu w(p_i c_i/w)$ must be the same for each agent, so that we may write

$$\varepsilon_i/\delta p_i = \lambda z_i \mathrm{var}(u_i/p_i)$$

where z_i is the proportion of aggregate wealth held in security i and λ is the risk aversion of a typical agent, that is of an agent who holds this proportion of his wealth in security i.

It is estimated by Grinblatt and Titman (1983) that the maximum levels of λ, z_i and $\mathrm{var}(u_i/p_i)$ are 10, 0.001 and 0.2 per year respectively, so that the annual maximum divergence of the expected return of a security from the level predicted by the linear return relation is 0.2 per cent per year.

BIBLIOGRAPHY

Chen, N., Roll, R. and Ross, S. (1986) 'Economic Forces and the Stock Market', *Journal of Business*, no 59, pp. 383–403.

Grinblatt, M. and Titman, S. (1983) 'Factor Pricing in a Finite Economy', *Journal of Financial Economics*, no 12, pp. 495–507.

Grinblatt, M. and Titman, S. (1987) 'The Relation between Mean-Variance Efficiency and Arbitrage Pricing', *Journal of Business*, no 60, pp. 97–112.

Huberman, G. (1982) 'A Simple Approach to Arbitrage Pricing', *Journal of Economic Theory*, no 28, pp. 183–91.

Huberman, G. (1989) 'Arbitrage Pricing Theory', in J. Eatwell, M. Milgate and P. Newman (eds) *The New Palgrave: Finance* (London: Macmillan).

Johnston, J. (1984) *Econometric Methods* (New York: McGraw-Hill) 3rd edn.

Lancaster, K. (1968) *Mathematical Economics* (Toronto: Macmillan).

Morrison, D. (1967) *Multivariate Statistical Methods* (New York: McGraw-Hill).

Roll, R. and Ross, S. (1980) 'An Empirical Investigation of the Arbitrage Pricing Theory', *Journal of Finance*, no 35, pp. 1073–103.

Roll, R. and Ross, S. (1984) 'The Arbitrage Pricing Approach to Strategic Planning', *Financial Analysts Journal*, no 40, pp. 14–26.

Ross, S. (1976) 'Return, Risk, and Arbitrage', in I. Friend and J. Bicksler (eds) *Risk and Return in Finance* (Cambridge: Ballinger).

Ross, S. (1976) 'The Arbitrage Theory of Capital Asset Pricing', *Journal of Economic Theory*, no 13, pp. 341–60.

Rubinstein, M. (1973) 'A Comparative Statics Analysis of Risk Premiums', *Journal of Business*, no 46, pp. 605–15.

Part III
Many Periods

5 Static Arbitrage: Forwards and Futures

This chapter extends the basic arbitrage theorem to a many-period setting. It commences by using static arbitrage to explain forward prices, and then proceeds to explain futures prices.

FORWARD CONTRACTS

We now extend the discussion from a single-period to a many-period setting. Since the essential differences may be illustrated by considering a single (risky) security and (risk-free) bonds we restrict our attention to these. Accordingly, we now use subscripts to denote dates rather than securities.

We consider contracts on a security whose payoff occurs on date s only. The price of this security on date t is denoted by p_t; since the sole payoff occurs on date s the price of the security (before the payoff is made) on this date, p_s, is simply the payoff of the security.

A forward contract (with maturity s) is a contract to buy the security on date s for the forward price prevailing when the contract was made. If the forward price on date t is denoted by g_t a forward contract made on date 0, say, is thus a security which specifies the receipt on date s of the amount $p_s - g_0$.

No payment is involved when a forward contract is made. Thus the forward price is not explicitly the price of a security; it is defined implicitly as the contract price at which the value of the forward contract when it is made is zero.

We assume that there exists a security with unit payoff on date s, that is a bond, the (necessarily positive) price on date t

of which is denoted by b_t. Equivalently, the $(s-t)$-period interest rate on date t is

$$1/b_t - 1.$$

Applying the martingale property to the forward contract on date 0 gives the value of this contract as

$$\hat{E}\delta(p_s - g_0)$$

where δ is the relevant discount factor and $\hat{E}$ the martingale expectation operator. Thus the forward price g_0 is defined by the condition

$$\hat{E}\delta(p_s - g_0) = 0.$$

Applying the martingale property to the security and to the bond gives

$$p_0 = \hat{E}\delta p_s$$

and

$$b_0 = \hat{E}\delta$$

respectively, so that

$$\hat{E}\delta(p_s - g_0) = p_0 - b_0 g_0 = 0,$$

and the forward price is given by

$$g_0 = p_0/b_0.$$

Equivalently, since p_0 is the price of a security whose payoff on date s is p_s, the forward price may be interpreted as the price of a security whose payoff on date s is p_s/b_0.

This result may be demonstrated more directly by considering the following strategy: on date 0 buy $1/b_0$ forwards and g_0/b_0 bonds. This is a static strategy in that all actions are determined on date 0. Since forward contracts involve no outlay the cost on date 0 is

$$b_0(g_0/b_0) = g_0,$$

and the payoff on date s is

$$(p_s - g_0)/b_0 + g_0/b_0 = p_s/b_0.$$

This is to say that g_0 is the price of a security whose payoff on date s is p_s/b_0.

Consider the example where the structure of discount factors is that illustrated in Figure 5.1 and all martingale probabilities are 0.5. Applying the martingale property recursively gives the structure of bond prices illustrated in Figure 5.2, so that

$$b_0 = 0.2.$$

Now consider a security whose payoff p_s in the four states is

$$(60, 40, 40, 10).$$

The structure of prices of this security is that illustrated in Figure 5.3, and the structure of prices of a security whose payoff is p_s/b_0 is that illustrated in Figure 5.4. As required,

$$g_0 = 40 = 8/0.2 = p_0/b_0.$$

Although the value of a new forward contract is by definition zero the value of an existing forward contract will not in general be zero. The value on date t of a forward contract made on date 0 is given by the martingale property as

$$p_t - b_t g_0,$$

or equivalently as

$$b_t(g_t - g_0).$$

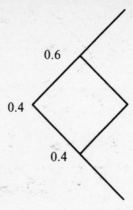

Figure 5.1

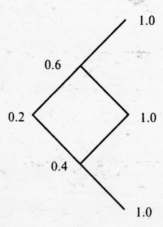

Figure 5.2

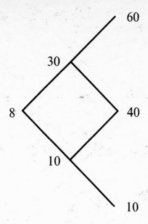

Figure 5.3

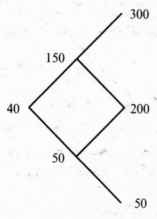

Figure 5.4

FUTURES CONTRACTS

A futures contract is similar to a forward contract but differs from this in that changes in the value of the contract are paid as they occur. More precisely, a futures contract (with maturity s) made on date 0, say, is a security which specifies the receipt on each date t from 1 to s of the amount $f_t - f_{t-1}$ where f_t, the futures price on date t, is the contract price at which the value of a futures contract made on date t is zero, and

$$f_s = p_s.$$

Thus futures prices are defined recursively: f_s is simply p_s; f_{s-1} is such that the value on date $s-1$ of the payoff $f_s - f_{s-1}$ on date s is zero; f_{s-2} is such that the value on date $s-2$ of the payoff $f_{s-1} - f_{s-2}$ on date $s-1$ is zero; and so forth. As with forward contracts, no payment is involved when a futures contract is made.

The total receipt specified by a futures contract made on date 0 is

$$(f_1 - f_0) + \ldots + (f_s - f_{s-1}) = f_s - f_0 = p_s - f_0,$$

that is, the difference between the security price on date s and the futures price on date 0. This total receipt is analogous to the receipt specified by a forward contract, which is the difference between the security price on date s and the forward price on date 0. However, the timing of the two receipts differs: the receipt specified by the forward contract occurs on date s only, while that specified by the futures contract may be spread over all dates from 1 to s.

We assume that on each date t there exists a security with unit payoff on date $t+1$, that is, a bill, the (necessarily positive) price of which is denoted by a_t (on date s the bill is 'instantaneous', its price being unity). Equivalently, the one-period interest rate on date t is

$$1/a_t - 1.$$

We denote by $z(t)$ the product of the t bill prices

$$a_0 \ldots a_{t-1}$$

(if t is positive, with $z(0)$ being defined as unity). The quantity $z(t)$ is the amount which if invested in bills on date 0 and continually reinvested until date $t-1$ produces a unit payoff on date t; equivalently,

$$1/z(t) - 1$$

is the t-period reinvestment rate on date 0.

Just as the forward price g_0 may be interpreted as the price of a security whose payoff on date s is p_s/b_0 the futures price f_0 may be interpreted as the price of a security whose payoff on date s is $p_s/z(s)$.

This result may be demonstrated by considering the following strategy: on each date t from 0 to $s-1$ buy

$$1/z(t+1) - 1/z(t)$$

futures and $f_t/z(t+1)$ bills. This is a dynamic strategy in that the action to be taken on each date depends on the prices on that date, and thus is not determined on date 0. It implies a holding after trading on date t of

$$(1/z(1) - 1/z(0)) + \ldots + (1/z(t+1) - 1/z(t))$$

$$= 1/z(t+1) - 1/z(0) = 1/z(t+1)$$

futures and of $f_t/z(t+1)$ bills. Since futures contracts involve no outlay the payment (for bills) involved on each date t from 1 to $s-1$ is

$$a_t f_t/z(t+1) = f_t/z(t)$$

and the corresponding receipt (from futures and bills) is

$$(f_t - f_{t-1})/z(t) + f_{t-1}/z(t) = f_t/z(t).$$

Thus the strategy involves no net payoffs from dates 1 to $s-1$. The cost on date 0 is

$$a_s f_0/z(1) = f_0/z(0) = f_0,$$

and the payoff on date s is

$$(f_s - f_{s-1})/z(s) + f_{s-1}/z(s) = f_s/z(s) = p_s/z(s).$$

This is to say that f_0 is the price of a security whose payoff on date s is $p_s/z(s)$.

This characterisation of futures prices allows us to determine the futures price using the martingale property. Noting that the relevant discount factor δ is the product of the one-period (risk-free) discount factors, that is $z(s)$, we have

$$f_0 = \hat{E}\delta p_s/z(s) = \hat{E}p_s,$$

so that the futures price is the expected value (under the martingale probabilities) of the security price on date s.

Consider the example discussed above where the structure of discount factors is that illustrated in Figure 5.1 and all martingale probabilities are 0.5 and where the security payoff in the four states is

$$(60, 40, 40, 10).$$

Then the quantity $z(s)$ in the four states is

$$(0.24, 0.24, 0.16, 0.16)$$

so that the structure of prices of a security whose payoff on date s is $p_s/z(s)$ is that illustrated in Figure 5.5. As required,

$$f_0 = 37.5 = \hat{E}p_s.$$

For future reference, the complete structure of futures prices is that illustrated in Figure 5.6.

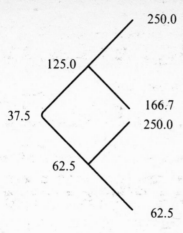

Figure 5.5

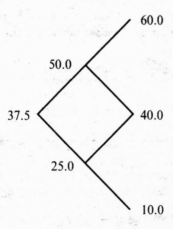

Figure 5.6

FORWARD–FUTURES EQUIVALENCE

In general, futures and forward prices differ because of the interrelation between discount factors, or interest rates, and security payoffs. However, if the two are independent (under the martingale probabilities), for example, because either one is deterministic, then futures and forward prices will be the same.

If discount factors are deterministic then applying the martingale property to the bond we have

$$b_0 = \hat{E}\delta = \hat{E}z(s) = z(s),$$

so that

$$p_s/b_0 = p_s/z(s).$$

Since g_0 is the price of a security whose payoff is p_s/b_0 and f_0 is the price of a security whose payoff is $p_s/z(s)$ it follows that

$$g_0 = f_0.$$

Similarly, if the payoff p_s is deterministic then applying the martingale property to a security whose payoff is p_s/b_0 we have

$$g_0 = \hat{E}z(s)p_s/b_0 = (p_s/b_0)\hat{E}z(s) = (p_s/b_0)b_0 = p_s$$

so that, since

$$f_0 = \hat{E}p_s = p_s,$$

we again have

$$g_0 = f_0.$$

This relationship between forward and futures prices, when either interest rates or security prices are deterministic, is known as the forward–futures equivalence principle.

Consider the example discussed above where all martingale probabilities are 0.5 and where the security payoff in the four states is

(60, 40, 40, 10),

but now where the structure of discount factors is that illustrated in Figure 5.7.

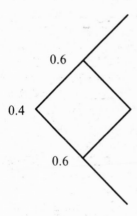

0.6

0.4

0.6

Figure 5.7

Since these discount factors are deterministic we have

$$b_0 = z(s) = 0.24$$

so that

$$p_0 = \delta \hat{E} p_0 = b_0 \hat{E} p_s = 9$$

and thus

$$g_0 = p_0/b_0 = 37.5 = \hat{E} p_s = f_0,$$

as required.

More generally, when discount factors, or equivalently bond prices, and security payoffs are not independent the futures price may be expected to be less than the forward price if bond prices are positively correlated with futures prices. This is because the holder of a futures contract will then expect to obtain interim receipts when bond prices are high, that is, when the benefit of investing such receipts is low, and will expect to make interim payments when bond prices are low, that is, when the cost of financing such payments is high. Since a forward contract involves no interim receipts or payments the futures price will have to be less than the forward price to prevent the forward contract from dominating the futures contract. Conversely, the futures price may be expected to exceed the forward price if bond prices are negatively correlated with futures prices.

The precise relation between forward and futures prices is obtained by interpreting the difference between the two as the price of a synthetic security. Consider the following strategy: on date 0 buy b_0 futures and sell a forward; and on each date t from 1 to $s-1$ buy $b_t - b_{t-1}$ futures and

$$(f_t - f_{t-1})b_{t-1}/b_t$$

bonds. This implies a holding after trading on date t of

$$b_0 + (b_1 - b_0) + \ldots + (b_t - b_{t-1}) = b_t$$

futures, of -1 forwards and of

$$(f_1 - f_0)b_0/b_1 + \ldots + (f_t - f_{t-1})b_{t-1}/b_t$$

bonds. Since forward and futures contracts involve no outlay the payment (for bonds) involved on each date t from 1 to $s-1$ is

$$b_t(f_t - f_{t-1})b_{t-1}/b_t = (f_t - f_{t-1})b_{t-1},$$

as is the corresponding receipt (from futures contracts). Thus the strategy involves no net payoffs from dates 1 to $s-1$. The cost on date 0 is zero, and the payoff on date s is

$$-(p_s-g_0)+(f_1-f_0)b_0/b_1+\ldots$$

$$+(f_{s-1}-f_{s-2})b_{s-2}/b_{s-1}+(f_s-f_{s-1})b_{s-1}$$

$$=-(p_s-g_0)+(f_1-f_0)b_0/b_1+\ldots+(f_s-f_{s-1})b_{s-1}/b_s,$$

noting that b_s is unity. This payoff may be written as

$$-(p_s-g_0)+f_s-f_0-v=g_0-f_0-v$$

where

$$v=(f_1-f_0)(b_1-b_0)/b_1+\ldots+(f_s-f_{s-1})(b_s-b_{s-1})/b_s.$$

This is to say that zero is the price of a security whose payoff on date s is

$$g_0-f_0-v=d_0-v,$$

say, so that zero is also the price of a security whose payoff is

$$d_0/b_0-v/b_0.$$

Since d_0 is the price of a security whose payoff is d_0/b_0 it follows that

$$d_0-0=d_0$$

is the price of a security whose payoff is

$$d_0/b_0-(d_0/b_0-v/b_0)=v/b_0.$$

Thus the difference between the forward and the futures price is the price of a synthetic security whose payoff on date s is v/b_0.

In a loose sense, if bond and futures prices are positively correlated on each date t then

$$(f_t - f_{t-1})(b_t - b_{t-1})$$

may be expected to be positive on each date t, so that

$$v = (f_1 - f_0)(b_1 - b_0)/b_1 + \ldots + (f_s - f_{s-1})(b_s - b_{s-1})/b_s$$

may also be expected to be positive. In this case d_0 is the price of a security whose payoff v/b_0 is positive so that d_0 is positive and the futures price is less than the forward price. Conversely, if bond and futures prices are negatively correlated on each date then the futures price may be expected to exceed the forward price.

A similar argument shows that if bond and forward prices are positively correlated on each date then the futures price may be expected to be less than the forward price, while if bond and forward prices are negatively correlated on each date then the futures price may be expected to exceed the forward price (see Cox, Ingersoll and Ross, 1981).

Consider the example discussed above where the structure of discount factors is that illustrated in Figure 5.1 and all martingale probabilities are 0.5, and where the security payoff p_s in the four states is

(60, 40, 40, 10).

Then the structures of bond and of futures prices are those illustrated in Figures 5.2 and 5.6 respectively, so that on date 1 (the only relevant date) bond and futures prices are positively correlated. The payoff v/b_0 of the synthetic security in the four states is

(61.7, 21.7, −76.3, 13.8),

so that the structure of synthetic security prices is that illustrated in Figure 5.8. As required,

$$d_0 = g_0 - f_0 = 2.5 > 0.$$

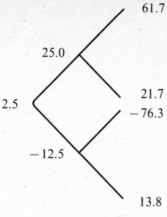

Figure 5.8

EVIDENCE

Tests of the relation between futures and forward prices are provided by French (1983), who investigates such prices for silver contracts with maturities of 3, 6 and 12 months. The means and t-statistics of the excess of the futures price over the forward price (expressed as a percentage) and of the covariance (multiplied by 10^7) between the daily percentage change of the futures price and that of the bond price are given in Table 5.1. It is only for the long (12-month) maturity that the covariance is significantly different from zero. For this maturity the covariance is negative, and, as required, the futures price is significantly greater than the forward price.

Table 5.1

		Excess	Covariance
3 months	Mean	0.1	3.2
	t-statistic	0.8	0.6
6 months	Mean	0.4	0.2
	t-statistic	2.3	0.0
12 months	Mean	0.8	− 19.5
	t-statistic	3.7	1.5

Tests of the relation between futures and spot prices are provided by MacKinlay and Ramaswamy (1988) who investigate actual and implied futures prices for a market index portfolio, where the implied futures price is derived from the spot price and the interest rate (assuming forward–futures equivalence and making an adjustment for dividends). This procedure is equivalent to comparing the discounted futures price with the spot price.

The mean and standard deviation, expressed as percentages, of the discrepancy between actual and implied futures prices, together with the first, second, third and fourth order serial correlations of this discrepancy with 15-minute intervals between observations, are given in Table 5.2. The mean is not significantly different from zero, but all serial correlations are high, indicating that although the discrepancy is small it is persistent.

Table 5.2

Mean	0.12
Standard deviation	0.44
Serial correlation 1	0.93
Serial correlation 2	0.91
Serial correlation 3	0.90
Serial correlation 4	0.98

Further evidence on the persistency of the discrepancy is obtained by specifying some arbitrary upper and lower bounds (0.6 and −0.6 per cent respectively) and considering all instances where the discrepancy crosses a bound, returns to zero and then again crosses some bound. The probability of the discrepancy crossing the upper bound given that it has previously crossed the lower bound and returned to zero is denoted by UL; the remaining three analogous conditional probabilities are denoted by UU, LU and LL. These probabilities are given in Table 5.3. The probability UU is significantly greater than UL, and the probability LL is significantly greater than LU, indicating a systematic persistency in the discrepancy.

Table 5.3

UL	0.36
UU	0.73
LU	0.27
LL	0.64

SYNTHETIC INDEXATION

Under the CAPM assumptions a mean-variance efficient portfolio is obtained as a linear combination of a risk-free portfolio and the market index portfolio, that is, by indexation of the risky component of the portfolio.

Such indexation may be obtained by replication, that is by holding all the constituents of the market portfolio, but this may involve significant transactions costs. These costs may be mitigated to some extent by sampling, that is, by holding only a representative sample of the constituents of the market portfolio, but this may involve tracking error, that is, a discrepancy between actual and index returns.

Alternatively, indexation may be obtained synthetically, that is, by holding bonds and index forwards or futures. If we denote the spot and forward prices of the index portfolio on date t by p_t and g_t respectively the total return of the index portfolio over the s periods is

$$p_s/p_0 - 1$$

and the corresponding return of a portfolio consisting of g_0 bonds and an index forward contract is

$$(g_0 + g_s - g_0)/b_0 g_0 - 1 = g_s/b_0 g_0 - 1 = p_s/p_0 - 1.$$

Thus the index return may be obtained synthetically using forward contracts; if forward–futures equivalence applies, for example because interest rates are deterministic, then the index return may also be obtained synthetically using futures contracts.

Synthetic indexation may be preferable to replication because the transactions costs for futures are substantially less than those for primary securities; it may be preferable to sampling because it involves only negligible tracking error.

BIBLIOGRAPHY

Black, F. (1976) 'The Pricing of Commodity Contracts', *Journal of Financial Economics*, no 3, pp. 167–79.

Cox, J. C., Ingersoll, J. E. and Ross, S. A. (1981) 'The Relation between Forward Prices and Futures Prices', *Journal of Financial Economics*, no 9, pp. 321–46.

French, K. (1983) 'A Comparison of Futures and Forward Prices', *Journal of Financial Economics*, no 12, pp. 311–42.

Jarrow, R. A. and Oldfield, G. S. (1981) 'Forward Contracts and Futures Contracts', *Journal of Financial Economics*, no 9, pp. 373–82.

MacKinlay, A. C. and Ramaswamy, K. (1988) 'Index-Futures Arbitrage and the Behavior of Stock Index Futures Prices', *The Review of Financial Studies*, no 1, pp. 137–58.

Richard, S. and Sundaresan, M. (1981) 'A Continuous Time Model of Forward and Futures Prices in a Multigood Economy', *Journal of Financial Economics*, no 9, pp. 347–72.

6 Dynamic Arbitrage: Options

This chapter continues the application of the basic arbitrage theorem in a many-period setting to value call and put options, and thus to value all derivative securities.

CALLS AND PUTS

We continue to consider contracts on a security whose payoff occurs on date s only, the price of which security on date t is denoted by p_t. We assume that the security is a limited liability security, so that p_t is positive on each date t.

A European call option (with maturity s and positive exercise price q), or a call, is a contract which gives its holder the right but not the obligation to buy the security on date s for the exercise price q. Similarly, a put gives its holder the right to sell the security on date s at the price q. The right involved in a call will be exercised if and only if the security price on date s exceeds the exercise price, that is, if and only if

$$p_s > q,$$

while the right involved in a put will be exercised if and only if

$$p_s < q.$$

Equivalently, then, the call is a security which specifies the receipt on date s of the amount $p_s - q$ if p_s exceeds q and a zero receipt otherwise, that is, which specifies the payoff

$$\max(p_s - q, 0)$$

119

on date s. Similarly, the put is a security which specifies the payoff

$$\max(q - p_s, 0)$$

on date s. The relation between the payoff of a call c_s and the security price at maturity p_s is illustrated in Figure 6.1; the corresponding relation for a put is illustrated in Figure 6.2.

We assume that there is a bond with unit payoff on date s, and also that on each date t there is a bill with unit payoff on date $t + 1$ (on date s the bill is 'instantaneous', its price being unity). Bond, bill, call, and put prices on date t are denoted by b_t, a_t, c_t, and d_t respectively.

Applying the martingale property to the call on date 0 gives

$$c_0 = \hat{E}\delta\max(p_s - q, 0) = \hat{E}\max(\delta p_s - \delta q, 0)$$

where δ is the relevant discount factor and $\hat{E}$ the martingale expectation operator, so that

$$c_0 + \hat{E}\delta q = \hat{E}\max(\delta p_s, \delta q).$$

Applying the martingale property to the put gives

$$d_0 = \hat{E}\delta\max(q - p_s, 0) = \hat{E}\max(\delta q - \delta p_s, 0),$$

so that

$$d_0 + \hat{E}\delta p_s = \hat{E}\max(\delta q, \delta p_s).$$

It follows that

$$c_0 + \hat{E}\delta q = c_0 + q\hat{E}\delta = d_0 + \hat{E}\delta p_s.$$

Now applying the martingale property to the bond and the security gives

$$b_0 = \hat{E}\delta$$

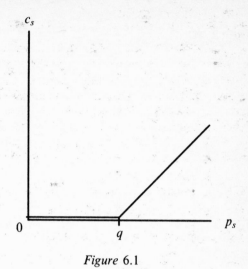

Figure 6.1

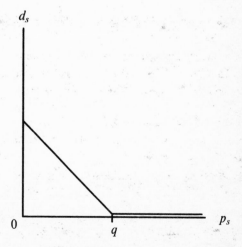

Figure 6.2

and

$$p_0 = \hat{E}\delta p_s$$

respectively, so that

$$c_0 + b_0 q = d_0 + p_0.$$

Thus the call price plus the discounted exercise price is equal to the put price plus the security price. This relation is known as put–call parity.

This result may be demonstrated more directly by considering the following strategy. On date 0 buy a call and q bonds, and sell a put and a security. The cost on date 0 is

$$c_0 + b_0 q - d_0 - p_0,$$

and the payoff on date s is

$$\max(p_s - q, 0) + q - \max(q - p_s, 0) - p_s$$

$$= \max(p_s, q) - \max(q, p_s) = 0.$$

Since the payoff is zero the cost must also be zero, so that

$$c_0 + b_0 q = d_0 + p_0.$$

The martingale property immediately restricts call prices. First,

$$c_0 = \hat{E}\max(\delta p_s - \delta q, 0) \geqslant \hat{E}(\delta p_s - \delta q)$$

$$= \hat{E}\delta p_s - \hat{E}\delta q = p_0 - b_0 q.$$

And second,

$$c_0 = \hat{E}\max(\delta p_s - \delta q, 0) \geqslant \hat{E}0 = 0.$$

Thus

$$c_0 \geqslant \max(p_0 - b_0 q, 0).$$

This property may be demonstrated more directly by considering the following strategies. First, buy a call and q bonds, and sell a security. The cost is

$$c_0 + b_0 q - p_0$$

and the payoff is

$$\max(p_s - q, 0) + q - p_s \geqslant 0.$$

Since the latter is non-negative the former must also be non-negative, so that

$$c_0 \geqslant p_0 - b_0 q.$$

Second, buy a call. The cost is c_0 and the payoff is

$$\max(p_s - q, 0) \geqslant 0.$$

Since the latter is non-negative the former must also be non-negative, so that

$$c_0 \geqslant 0.$$

Further,

$$p_s - \max(p_s - q, 0) = \min(p_s, q) > 0$$

so that

$$\hat{E}\delta p_s - \hat{E}\delta \max(p_s - q, 0) = p_0 - c_0 > 0,$$

and

$$c_0 < p_0.$$

This property may also be demonstrated more directly. Consider buying a security and selling a call. The cost of this strategy is $p_0 - c_0$ and the payoff is

$$p_s - \max(p_s - q, 0) = \min(p_s, q) > 0.$$

Since the latter is positive the former must also be positive, so that

$$c_0 < p_0.$$

The call price boundary conditions,

$$\max(p_0 - b_0 q, 0) \leqslant c_0 < p_0,$$

are illustrated in Figure 6.3.

Similar restrictions on put prices may be obtained analogously. Equivalently, using put–call parity, we have

$$d_0 = c_0 + b_0 q - p_0 \geqslant (p_0 - b_0 q) + b_0 q - p_0 = 0,$$

$$d_0 = c_0 + b_0 q - p_0 \geqslant 0 + b_0 q - p_0 = b_0 q - p_0$$

and

$$d_0 = c_0 + b_0 q - p_0 < p_0 + b_0 q - p_0 = b_0 q.$$

The put price boundary conditions,

$$\max(b_0 q - p_0, 0) \leqslant d_0 < b_0 q,$$

are illustrated in Figure 6.4.

Consider the example where the structure of discount factors is that illustrated in Figure 6.5 and all martingale probabilities are 0.5. Applying the martingale property recursively gives the structure of bond prices illustrated in Figure 6.6, so that

$$b_0 = 0.2.$$

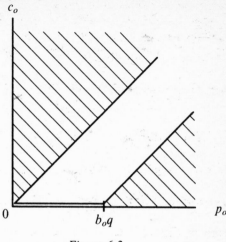

Figure 6.3

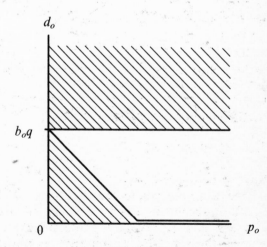

Figure 6.4

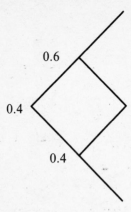

Figure 6.5

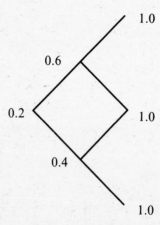

Figure 6.6

Now consider a security whose payoff p_s in the four states is

(60, 40, 40, 10).

The structure of security prices is that illustrated in Figure 6.7, so that

$p_0 = 8$.

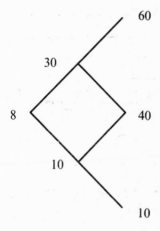

Figure 6.7

The payoff in the four states of a call on this security with an exercise price q of 30 is

(30, 10, 10, 0),

so that the structure of call prices is that illustrated in Figure 6.8, and

$c_0 = 2.8$.

As required,

$\max(p_0 - b_0 q, 0) = 2 \leqslant 2.8 < 8 = p_0.$

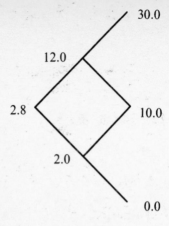

Figure 6.8

Similarly, the payoff in the four states of a put with the same exercise price is

(0, 0, 0, 20),

so that the structure of put prices is that illustrated in Figure 6.9,

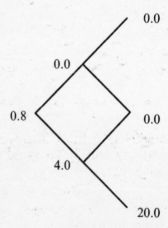

Figure 6.9

and

$$d_0 = 0.8.$$

As required,

$$\max(b_0 q - p_0, 0) = 0 \leqslant 0.8 < 6 = b_0 q.$$

Also,

$$c_0 + b_0 q = 8.8 = d_0 + p_0,$$

as required by put–call parity.

A PRICING FORMULA

We may obtain an explicit option pricing formula in the case where the interest rate is constant and the price of the underlying security follows a binomial random walk. In this case for each date t (prior to s) we have

$$a_t = \delta$$

and either

$$p_{t+1} = \alpha p_t$$

or

$$p_{t+1} = \beta p_t$$

for some given parameters δ (now interpreted as the one-period discount factor), α and β. To avoid trivial arbitrage possibilities we assume that

$$0 < \alpha < 1/\delta < \beta.$$

This assumption precludes, for example, our considering options on bonds for which, as the interest rate is constant,

$$b_{t+1} = b_t/\delta$$

and thus

$$\alpha = 1/\delta = \beta.$$

The structure of security prices between dates t and $t+1$ is that illustrated in Figure 6.10.

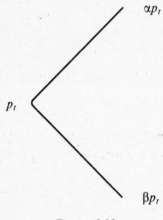

Figure 6.10

Applying the martingale property to the security on some date t gives

$$p_t = \delta[\pi\alpha p_t + (1-\pi)\beta p_t]$$

where π is the martingale probability of an upward move, that is, of the occurrence

$$p_{t+1} = \alpha p_t.$$

It follows from this condition that

$$\pi = (1/\delta - \beta)/(\alpha - \beta).$$

The martingale probability of any one state in which there are u upward moves and $s-u$ downward moves is

$$\pi^u(1-\pi)^{s-u},$$

and in any such state we have

$$p_s = \alpha^u\beta^{s-u}p_0 = \theta(u),$$

say. Given some positive integer h we denote by $h!$ the product of the h integers

$$1 \ldots h,$$

and define $0!$ to be unity. Since there are

$$s!/u!(s-u)! = \lambda(u),$$

say, states in which there are u upward moves and $s-u$ downward moves the martingale probability of obtaining

$$p_s = \theta(u)$$

is

$$\lambda(u)\pi^u(1-\pi)^{s-u} = \mu(u),$$

say.

Applying the martingale property to a call (with maturity s and exercise price q) gives

$$c_0 = \delta^s\hat{E}c_s$$

$$= \delta^s[\mu(0)\max(\theta(0)-q,\ 0) + \ldots + \mu(s)\max(\theta(s)-q,\ 0)].$$

Let v be the smallest non-negative integer such that $\theta(v)$ exceeds q. If u is less than v then

$$\max(\theta(u)-q,\ 0) = 0$$

while if u is greater than or equal to v then

$$\max(\theta(u) - q, 0) = \theta(u) - q.$$

We may then write

$$c_0 = \delta^s [\mu(v)(\theta(v) - q) + \ldots + \mu(s)(\theta(s) - q)]$$

$$= [\delta^s \mu(v)\theta(v) + \ldots + \delta^s \mu(s)\theta(s)] - \delta^s q[\mu(v) + \ldots + \mu(s)].$$

Now

$$\delta^s \mu(u)\theta(u) = \delta^s \lambda(u)\pi^u (1 - \pi)^{s-u} \alpha^u \beta^{s-u} p_0$$

$$= \lambda(u)(\delta\alpha\pi)^u [\delta\beta(1 - \pi)]^{s-u} p_0$$

$$= \lambda \pi'^u (1 - \pi')^{s-u} p_0 = \mu'(u)p_0,$$

say, where

$$\pi' = \delta\alpha\pi,$$

noting that

$$1 - \pi' = 1 - \delta\alpha\pi = (\delta\alpha\beta - \beta)/(\alpha - \beta) = \delta\beta(1 - \pi).$$

Thus we may write

$$c_0 = p_0[\mu'(v) + \ldots + \mu'(s)] - \delta^s q[\mu(v) + \ldots + \mu(s)].$$

The sum

$$\mu(v) + \ldots + \mu(s)$$

is the probability of obtaining at least v upward moves out of s when the probability of each upward move is π. This sum is written as

$$C(v, s, \pi),$$

C being the complementary binomial distribution function. Similarly, the sum

$$\mu'(v) + \ldots + \mu'(s)$$

is written as

$$C(v, s, \pi').$$

We may then express the call price c_0 in terms of the parameters s, q, p_0, δ, α and β as

$$c_0 = p_0 C(v, s, \pi') - \delta^s q C(v, s, \pi)$$

where v is the smallest non-negative integer such that

$$\alpha^v \beta^{s-v} p_0 > q,$$

$$\pi = (1/\delta - \beta)/(\alpha - \beta)$$

and

$$\pi' = \delta \alpha \pi.$$

This expression is known as the binomial call-price formula; the corresponding put-price formula is obtained from this using put–call parity.

The binomial call-price formula may also be obtained more directly. We denote the call price on date t given the security price p_t by $c_t(p_t)$, and consider the following strategy: on date t buy

$$h_t(p_t) = [c_{t+1}(\alpha p_t) - c_{t+1}(\beta p_t)]/(\alpha - \beta)p_t$$

securities and

$$k_t(p_t) = [\alpha c_{t+1}(\beta p_t) - \beta c_{t+1}(\alpha p_t)]/(\alpha - \beta)$$

bills; and on date $t+1$ sell $h_t(p_t)$ securities. The cost of this strategy on date t is

$$p_t h_t(p_t) + \delta k_t(p_t);$$

the payoff on date $t+1$ is

$$\alpha p_t h_t(p_t) + k_t(p_t) = [\alpha c_{t+1}(\alpha p_t) - \beta c_{t+1}(\alpha p_t)]/(\alpha - \beta)$$

$$= c_{t+1}(\alpha p_t)$$

if the security price is αp_t and

$$\beta p_t h_t(p_t) + k_t(p_t) = [\alpha c_{t+1}(\beta p_t) - \beta c_{t+1}(\beta p_t)]/(\alpha - \beta)$$

$$= c_{t+1}(\beta p_t)$$

if the security price is βp_t.

Thus the payoff of the strategy is the same as that of holding a call, so that the cost of the strategy must be the same as that of a call, which is to say that

$$c_t = p_t h_t(p_t) + \delta k_t(p_t).$$

This expression gives c_t in terms of p_t, $c_{t+1}(\alpha p_t)$ and $c_{t+1}(\beta p_t)$. Now

$$c_s(\alpha p_{s-1}) = \max(\alpha p_{s-1} - q, 0)$$

and

$$c_s(\beta p_{s-1}) = \max(\beta p_{s-1} - q, 0),$$

so that c_{s-1} is determined for each value of p_{s-1}. Repeating this procedure a further $s-1$ times produces an expression for c_0 in terms of p_0, which expression is the binomial call-price formula (see Cox, Ross and Rubinstein, 1979).

In this approach the quantity $h_t(p_t)$ is the call hedge ratio on date t given the security price p_t; this ratio is the amount of the security which must be sold on date t to obtain a risk-free payoff on date $t+1$ if a call has been bought. Similarly, the put hedge ratio on date t is the amount of the security which must be bought on date t to obtain a risk-free payoff on date $t+1$ if a put has been bought.

Consider the example where the parameters s, q, p_0, δ, α and β are 2, 5, 10, 0.8, 2 and 0.5 respectively. Then

$$\pi = 0.5,$$

$$\pi' = 0.8$$

and

$$v = 1$$

so that

$$c_0 = 10C(1, 2, 0.8) - 3.2C(1, 2, 0.5)$$

$$= 10 * 0.96 - 3.2 * 0.75 = 7.2.$$

The structure of call hedge ratios implicit in this approach is that illustrated in Figure 6.11.

This result is confirmed by the recursive approach. The structure of security prices is that illustrated in Figure 6.12.

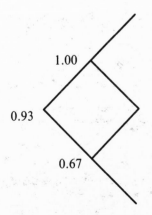

Figure 6.11

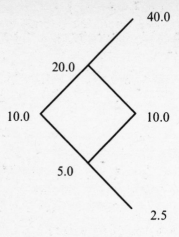

Figure 6.12

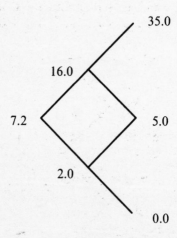

Figure 6.13

Then since all discount factors are 0.8 all martingale probabilities π of upward moves must be such that

$$1 = 0.8[2.0\pi + 0.5(1 - \pi)],$$

that is, all martingale probabilities must be 0.5, so that the structure of call prices is that illustrated in Figure 6.13, and

$$c_0 = 7.2.$$

It is instructive to consider the effect of increasing the number of periods while decreasing the duration of each so that the total duration remains unchanged. We thus choose some positive integer h and consider hs periods each of duration $1/h$ instead of s periods each of duration unity. We also specify the parameters δ, α and β in such a way that the overall discount factor and, for arbitrary probabilities, the mean and variance of the security return over the total duration are independent of how this duration is subdivided, that is, are independent of h.

One way to achieve this property (see Cox, Ross and Rubinstein, 1979) is to specify

$$\delta = \gamma^{s/h},$$

$$\alpha = \exp[\sigma/\sqrt{(s/h)}]$$

$$\beta = \exp[-\sigma/\sqrt{(s/h)}]$$

where γ is the discount factor for some fixed unit of time and σ is the volatility of the security return for this fixed unit of time, that is

$$\sigma^2 u = \text{var}[\log(p_{t+u}/p_t)]$$

where the function log is defined by

$$\log(\exp(\varepsilon)) = \varepsilon.$$

We investigate the behaviour of the call price as the number of periods becomes large, or equivalently as the duration of each period becomes small. In the limit as h tends to infinity the binomial random walk converges to a continuous random walk. Also, the complementary binomial value

$$C(v, s, \pi)$$

converges to $N(x)$ where N is the normal distribution function (see Morrison, 1967; 1.3) and

$$x = \log(p_0/\delta^s q)/\sigma\sqrt{s} + \sigma\sqrt{s}/2;$$

similarly,

$$C(v, s, \pi')$$

converges to

$$N(x - \sigma\sqrt{s})$$

(see Cox, Ross and Rubinstein, 1979). We may then express the limiting call price c_0 in terms of the parameters s, q, p_0, δ and σ as

$$c_0 = p_0 N(x) - \delta^s q N(x - \sigma\sqrt{s})$$

where

$$x = \log(p_0/\delta^s q)/\sigma\sqrt{s} + \sigma\sqrt{s}/2.$$

This expression is known as the Black–Scholes call-price formula; the corresponding put-price formula is obtained from this using put–call parity. These formulas may alternatively be derived directly from the assumption that the security price follows a continuous random walk using continuous time arbitrage arguments; in this approach the call hedge ratio at time t, given the price p_t, is $N(x)$ (see Black and Scholes, 1973).

We return to the example where the parameters s, p_0, δ, α and β are 2, 10, 0.8, 2 and 0.5 respectively. The call prices (for three values of q) given by the binomial formula for various values of h, and by the Black–Scholes formula (with

$$\sigma = \log(2) = 0.69),$$

are given in Table 6.1.

Table 6.1

h	$q = 5$	$q = 10$	$q = 15$
1	7.12	5.39	3.66
2	7.20	4.80	4.00
4	7.21	5.02	4.07
8	7.15	5.15	4.07
16	7.23	5.29	4.04
32	7.21	5.27	4.01
64	7.23	5.30	4.06
128	7.24	5.33	4.05
B–S	7.24	5.33	4.06

As required, the binomial values converge to the Black–Scholes values as the number of intervals h becomes large.

AMERICAN OPTIONS

American options differ from European options in that they may be exercised on any date up to (and including) the maturity date. Thus an American call (with maturity s and exercise price q) gives its holder the right to buy the underlying security on any date up to the maturity date s for the exercise price q. Similarly, an American put gives its holder the right to sell the security on any date up to s for the price q.

We denote the price on date t of the American call and put by c_t^* and d_t^* respectively. Since an American call may be exercised prematurely its value on date t cannot be less than its immediate exercise value, that is

$$c_t^* \geqslant p_t - q.$$

However, the call will only be exercised on date t if there is no value lost by such exercise, that is if

$$c_t^* = p_t - q.$$

Similarly,

$$d_t^* \geqslant q - p_t$$

and a put will only be exercised on date t if

$$d_t^* = q - p_t.$$

Since an American option contains all the rights contained in the corresponding European option its value cannot be less than the value of this corresponding European option, so that

$$c_t^* \geqslant c_t$$

and

$$d_t^* \geqslant d_t.$$

Then since

$$c_t^* \geqslant c_t \geqslant p_t - b_t q > p_t - q$$

on each date t prior to s the call will never be exercised prematurely. Its value, therefore, must be the same as that of a corresponding European call, so that

$$c_t^* = c_t.$$

It follows that all the properties developed for European calls apply to American calls. In particular, we have the boundary conditions

$$\max(p_0 - b_0 q, \, 0) \leqslant c_0^* < p_0,$$

and the binomial call-price formula applies if interest rates are constant and security prices follow a binomial random walk.

Similarly, we have

$$d_0^* \geqslant d_0 \geqslant \max(b_0 q - p_0, \, 0)$$

as a lower bound for the American put price. To specify an upper bound consider the following strategy: on date 0 acquire q dollars and sell an American put; if the put is exercised then at that time dispose of q dollars and buy a security. The cost of this strategy on date 0 is $q - d_0^*$. If the put is exercised on date t then the additional cost on that date is

$$q - p_t - q + p_t = 0$$

and the payoff on date s is p_s. If the put is not exercised then the payoff on date s is q. Since both possible payoffs are positive the cost must also be positive, so that

$$d_0^* < q.$$

We thus have the boundary conditions

$$\max(b_0 q - p_0, \, 0) \leqslant d_0^* < q.$$

However, although these imply that

$$d_t^* \geqslant b_t q - p_t$$

for each date t it does not follow from this that

$$d_t^* > q - p_t,$$

so that we cannot exclude premature exercise.

Indeed, the American put price will always exceed the European, implying premature exercise, if the exercise price is sufficiently high. Consider the case where the exercise price is equal to the highest possible security price on date s (noting that as there are only a finite number of states there are only a finite number of such prices). Then a call is of no value, so that

$$d_0 = c_0 + b_0 q - p_0 = b_0 q - p_0.$$

But

$$d_0^* \geqslant q - p_0 > b_0 q - p_0$$

so that

$$d_0^* > d_0$$

and the American put price exceeds the European.

Since d_0^* may exceed d_0 while c_0^* is the same as c_0 put–call parity will not in general apply to American options; nor, therefore, will the binomial put pricing formula.

However, we have

$$c_0^* + b_0 q = c_0 + b_0 q = d_0 + p_0 \leqslant d_0^* + p_0$$

as one bound for the relation between American put and call prices. To specify the other bound consider the following strategy: on date 0 acquire q dollars, buy a call, and sell an American put and a security; if the put is exercised then at that time dispose of q dollars and buy a security. The cost of this strategy on date 0 is

$$q + c_0^* - d_0^* - p_0.$$

If the put is exercised on date t then the additional cost on that date is

$$q - p_t - q + p_t = 0$$

and the payoff on date s is

$$\max(p_s - q, 0) \geqslant 0.$$

If the put is not exercised then the payoff on date s is

$$q + \max(p_s - q, 0) - \max(q - p_s, 0) - p_s = 0.$$

Since both possible payoffs are non-negative the cost must also be non-negative, so that

$$c_0^* + q \geqslant d_0^* + p_0.$$

We thus have the American put–call restrictions

$$c_0^* + b_0 q \leqslant d_0^* + p_0 \leqslant c_0^* + q.$$

Consider the example discussed above where the structure of discount factors is that illustrated in Figure 6.5 and all martingale probabilities are 0.5, and where the security payoff in the four states is

$$(60, 40, 40, 10)$$

and the exercise price is 30. The structure of European call prices c_t is that illustrated in Figure 6.8 and the structure of immediate call exercise values $p_t - q$ is that illustrated in Figure 6.14. Since

$$c_t > p_t - q$$

at each node (prior to date s) the call is not exercised prematurely, so that

$$c_0^* = c_0 = 2.8.$$

The structure of European put prices d_t is that illustrated in Figure 6.9 and the structure of immediate put exercise values $q - p_t$ is that illustrated in Figure 6.15. Since we do not have

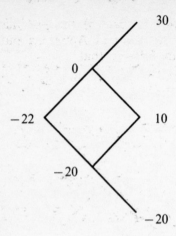

Figure 6.14

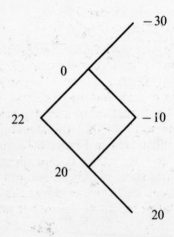

Figure 6.15

$$d_t > q - p_t$$

at each node (prior to date s) the put may be exercised prematurely. The structure of American put prices is that illustrated in Figure 6.16, so that

$$d_0^* = 22 > 0.8 = d_0.$$

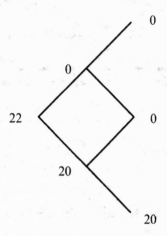

Figure 6.16

In this example the American put is always exercised prematurely. A more interesting example is obtained by taking all discount factors to be 0.9 (rather than those illustrated in Figure 6.5) and the exercise price to be 34 (rather than 30). The structure of security prices is now that illustrated in Figure 6.17 so that the structure of European put prices is that illustrated in Figure 6.18 and the structure of immediate put exercise values is that illustrated in Figure 6.19. Then the structure of American put prices is that illustrated in Figure 6.20. In this example the put is exercised prematurely (on date 1) in some states but not in others. As required,

$$d_0^* = 5.2 > 4.9 = d_0.$$

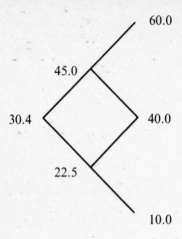

Figure 6.17

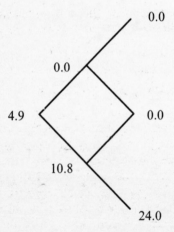

Figure 6.18

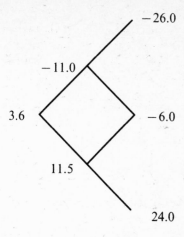

Figure 6.19

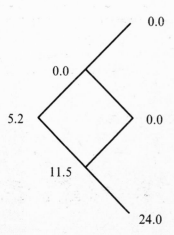

Figure 6.20

FUTURES OPTIONS

Options may be defined on any underlying security (including options themselves). They may also be defined on the futures (or forward) price, even though this is not the price of a security.

A European futures call option (with maturity s and exercise price q) gives its holder the right to acquire a futures contract, with maturity s and contract price q, on date s. Such an option will only be exercised if the value of the futures contract on date s is positive, that is, denoting the futures price on date t by f_t, if

$$f_s - q = p_s - q > 0.$$

Equivalently, then, the futures call is a security whose payoff on date s is

$$\max(p_s - q, 0) = c_s,$$

so that a European futures call is identical to a securities call.

Similarly, a European put option gives its holder the right to dispose of a futures contract, with maturity s and contract price q, on date s. This is identical to a (European) securities put.

We assume that forward–futures equivalence applies, for example, because interest rates are deterministic. Then the futures price f_t on date t is equal to the forward price, which in turn is equal to p_t/b_t. Accordingly,

$$c_0 + b_0 q = d_0 + b_0 f_0.$$

so that the call price plus the discounted exercise price is equal to the put price plus the discounted futures price. This relation is known as futures put–call parity.

Consider the case where (one-period) discount rates are constant, at δ, and the security price follows a binomial random walk with upward and downward moves of α and β respectively. Then since

$$f_{t+1}/f_t = (p_{t+1}/\delta^{s-t-1})/(p_t/\delta^{s-t}) = \delta p_{t+1}/p_t$$

the futures price follows a binomial random walk with upward and downward moves of

$$\delta\alpha = \lambda$$

and

$$\delta\beta = \mu,$$

say, respectively.

We may then express the European futures call price c_0 in terms of the futures parameters f_0, λ and μ by replacing p_0, α and β in the binomial call-price formula by $\delta^s f_0$, λ/δ and μ/δ respectively. This gives

$$c_0 = \delta^s[f_0 C(v, s, \pi') - qC(v, s, \pi)]$$

where v is the smallest non-negative integer such that

$$\lambda^v \mu^{s-v} f_0 > q,$$

$$\pi = (1-\mu)/(\lambda-\mu)$$

and

$$\pi' = \lambda\pi.$$

The corresponding expression for the European futures put price is obtained from this using futures put–call parity.

Now

$$\log(f_{t+1}/f_t) = \log(\delta p_{t+1}/p_t) = \log(p_{t+1}/p_t) + \log(\delta)$$

so that

$$\mathrm{var}[\log(f_{t+1}/f_t)] = \mathrm{var}[\log(p_{t+1}/p_t)] = \sigma^2,$$

which is to say that the volatility of the futures price is the same as that of the security price. We may then express the European futures call price in the limiting case of a continuous random walk in terms of the futures price f_0 simply by replacing p_0 in the Black–Scholes call-price formula by $\delta^s f_0$. This gives

$$c_0 = \delta^s[f_0 N(y) - q N(y - \sigma/\sqrt{s})]$$

where

$$y = \log(f_0/q)/\sigma\sqrt{s} + \sigma\sqrt{s}/2.$$

Again, the corresponding expression for the European futures put price is obtained from this using futures put–call parity.

Although European futures options are identical to European securities options American futures options differ from American securities options. If an American futures call is exercised on date t the exerciser acquires a futures contract with a contract price of q. Since changes in the value of a futures contract are payable immediately he thus acquires an immediate payoff of $f_t - q$ (together with a new futures contract whose value, by definition, is zero). Similarly, if an American put is exercised on date t the exerciser acquires an immediate payoff of $q - f_t$.

An American futures call will only be exercised on date t if its value is equal to its immediate payoff. Since this value cannot be less than the value of a corresponding European call, that is c_t, the American call may be exercised on date t if

$$f_t - q \geqslant c_t \geqslant p_t - b_t q = b_t(f_t - q),$$

that is to say, as

$$0 < b_t < 1,$$

if

$$f_t \geqslant q.$$

American futures calls, unlike American securities calls, may then be exercised prematurely. It follows that the binomial and Black–Scholes pricing formulas do not apply to American futures calls.

Similarly, an American futures put will only be exercised on date t if

$$f_t \leqslant q.$$

American futures puts, as American securities puts, may also be exercised prematurely.

Consider again the example where all discount factors are 0.9 (so that forward–futures equivalence applies) and all martingale probabilities are 0.5, and where the security payoff in the four states is

$$(60, 40, 40, 10)$$

and the exercise price is 34. The structure of security prices is that illustrated in Figure 6.17 so that the structure of futures prices is that illustrated in Figure 6.21.

Then the structure of European futures call prices c_t is that illustrated in Figure 6.22 and the structure of immediate futures call exercise values $f_t - q$ is that illustrated in Figure 6.23. Since we do not have

$$c_t > f_t - q$$

at each node the futures call may be exercised prematurely. The structure of American futures call prices is that illustrated in Figure 6.24, so that the American futures call price of 8.40 exceeds the European call price of 7.70.

However, a similar argument demonstrates that the American futures put is not exercised prematurely, so that the American futures put price is the same as the European futures put price, both being 4.9.

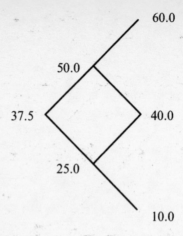

Figure 6.21

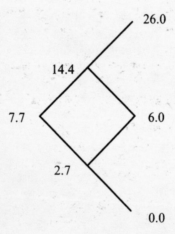

Figure 6.22

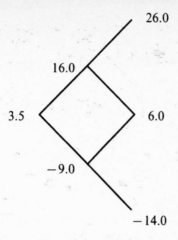

Figure 6.23

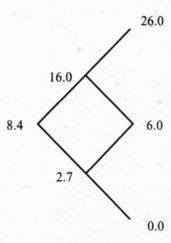

Figure 6.24

CORPORATE SECURITIES REVISITED

In Chapter 2 we considered a company financed by debt maturing on date s with a (positive) nominal value of q (using the notation of the present chapter) and equity. If the (positive) value of the company on date t is denoted by p_t the payoff on date s of debt is

$$\min(p_s, q) = q - \max(q - p_s, 0)$$

and that of equity is

$$\max(p_s - q, 0).$$

Both debt and equity may then be interpreted as (European) options on the value of the company with maturity s and exercise price q. Buying debt is equivalent to buying q bonds and selling a put, while buying equity is equivalent to buying a call.

We denote the prices on date t of debt and equity by u_t and v_t respectively, and the prices of a call and a put on the value of the company by c_t and d_t respectively. Then

$$u_0 = b_0 q - d_0$$

and

$$v_0 = c_0,$$

so that, using put–call parity,

$$p_0 = u_0 + v_0.$$

This relation between debt and equity prices is, effectively, the Modigliani–Miller irrelevancy proposition, which proposition is thus equivalent to the put–call parity relation.

We assume that (one-period) discount rates are constant, at δ, and that the value of the company follows a binomial random walk. (This implies that the equity price, being the price of a call on the value of the company, does not follow a binomial random walk.) Then the prices of calls and puts on the value of the company, and thus of debt and equity, are given by the binomial pricing formulas, or, in the limiting case of a continuous random walk, by the Black–Scholes formulas. (However, the prices of options on the equity are not given by such formulas.)

In the limiting case of a continuous random walk, with volatility σ, we have

$$v_0 = p_0 N(x) - \delta^s q N(x - \sigma\sqrt{s})$$

and

$$u_0 = p_0 - u_0 = p_0[1 - N(x)] + \delta^s q N(x - \sigma\sqrt{s})$$

where

$$x = \log(p_0/\delta^s q)/\sigma\sqrt{s} + \sigma\sqrt{s}/2.$$

These two equations give the values of equity, u_0, and debt, v_0, in terms of the value of the company, p_0. Together they specify the relation between v_0 and u_0, or equivalently between v_0/q and u_0/q, that is between the equity price and the debt price each expressed as a proportion of the nominal debt.

Consider the example where the parameters s, δ and σ are 1, 0.8 and 1 respectively. The debt price for various levels of equity price, each expressed as a proportion of the nominal debt, are given in Table 6.2.

Table 6.2

Equity	Debt
0.0	0.00
0.5	0.55
1.0	0.64
1.5	0.68
2.0	0.71
∞	0.80

In the limiting case where there is no equity debt is worthless, while in the other limiting case, as equity becomes infinite, the debt price approaches the bond price; between these two limits the value of debt increases as the value of equity increases.

More complicated corporate securities, such as warrants and convertibles, may be valued using similar arguments. Rather than considering each of the possibilities individually we show that any (European) derivative security, that is any security whose payoff on date s is a function of the value of the company on that date, may be interpreted as a portfolio consisting of calls with various exercise prices on the value of the company and bonds (or, equivalently, of calls and puts).

Consider an arbitrary derivative security whose payoff on date s is $h(p_s)$, where h is some given function. Simple examples of such a security are forwards, calls and puts (with a contract or exercise price of q); in these examples the function h is defined by

$$h(z) = z - q,$$

$$h(z) = \max(z - q, \, 0)$$

and

$$h(z) = \max(q - z, \, 0)$$

respectively.

We denote the possible values of p_s by

$$p^1, \ldots, p^m,$$

where the indices are chosen so that

$$p^1 < \ldots < p^m$$

(noting that as there are only a finite number of states there are only a finite number of such values). For each outcome j (other than m) we define

$$\lambda^j = (h^{j+1} - h^j)/(p^{j+1} - p^j)$$

where

$$h^j = h(p^j).$$

Consider a portfolio consisting of h^1 bonds, λ^1 calls with an exercise price of p^1 and, for each outcome j (other than 1 and m), $\lambda^{j+1} - \lambda^j$ calls with an exercise price of p^{j+1}. If the outcome k occurs the payoff of this portfolio is

$$h^1 + \lambda^1(p^k - p^1) + (\lambda^2 - \lambda^1)(p^k - p^2) + \ldots$$

$$+ (\lambda^{k-1} - \lambda^{k-2})(p^k - p^{k-1})$$

$$= h^1 + \lambda^1(p^2 - p^1) + \ldots + \lambda^{k-1}(p^k - p^{k-1})$$

$$= h^1 + (h^2 - h^1) + \ldots + (h^k - h^{k-1}) = h^k.$$

Since this applies for any outcome k the payoff of the portfolio of bonds and calls is $h(p_s)$, that is the payoff of the derivative security. It follows that the derivative security is equivalent to a portfolio of calls and bonds.

If bonds are not available then the same payoff may be obtained from a portfolio consisting of calls and puts. This is achieved by replacing the purchase of h^1 bonds with the purchase of a call with an exercise price of zero (which is equivalent to the purchase of a security), the purchase of a put with an exercise price of h^1 and the sale of a call with an exercise price of h^1, the payoff of which portfolio is

$$p_s + \max(h^1 - p_s, 0) - \max(p_s - h^1, 0) = h^1.$$

EVIDENCE

Tests of the options boundary conditions are provided by Galai (1978). The two call boundary conditions

$$c_0 \geqslant 0$$

and

$$c_0 < p_0$$

naturally present no problems. Galai examines the remaining call boundary condition,

$$c_0 \geqslant p_0 - b_0 q$$

(with an adjustment for dividends), for a number of securities and finds it to be satisfied in 94 per cent of the cases where it is relevant, that is where

$$p_0 > b_0 q.$$

In the cases where this condition is not satisfied the deviation is small: as is shown by Phillips and Smith (1978), it is less than even the lowest transactions costs.

Tests of the Black–Scholes formulas, which require that security prices follow a continuous random walk, are provided by Chiras and Manaster (1978). The immediate difficulty which arises in testing these formulas is that while the maturity s, discount factor δ, security price p_0 and exercise price q are known the volatility σ is not. To avoid this difficulty Chiras and Manaster consider a number of call options, with different maturities or exercise prices, on the same security and calculate the implied volatilities of each, that is the values of σ which satisfy the Black–Scholes call price formula given the call price c_0 and the remaining parameters s, δ, p_0 and q. If the Black–Scholes formula applies then all implied volatilities should be the same. However, for approximately a quarter of the securities considered the highest implied volatility exceeds the lowest by at least 20 per cent.

To assess the significance of these differences a (weighted) average of the implied volatilities is used to calculate implied prices for each of the options using the Black–Scholes formula. The following strategy is then adopted: hold a long position in the call whose implied price exceeds its actual price by the greatest percentage, and a short position in the call whose actual price exceeds its implied price by the greatest percentage, provided that both such percentages exceed 10; in each case the number of calls held is the inverse of their hedge ratio.

If the Black–Scholes formula applies approximately the payoff of this strategy, which is designed to be risk-free, should be small. In fact, the strategy is profitable in only 79 per cent of the cases, and the profits obtained are small: as is shown by Phillips and Smith (1978), they are less than the transactions costs involved.

PORTFOLIO INSURANCE

Consider the holder of a portfolio with a value of p_0 who buys a (European) put on this portfolio with maturity s and exercise price p_0 (that is, an at-the-money put) for the put price d_0 and sells d_0/b_0 bonds. If p_s is less than p_0 his payoff on date s is

$$p_0 - d_0/b_0$$

while if p_s is greater than p_0 his payoff is

$$p_s - d_0/b_0.$$

By adopting this strategy he thus insures against the value of his portfolio falling by more than d_0/p_0 while retaining the benefit of any increase above d_0/b_0 in the value of his portfolio; the effective premium payable (in advance) for this insurance is the put price d_0. The relation between the value at maturity of his insured portfolio, w, and that of his original portfolio, p_s, is illustrated in Figure 6.25.

As an alternative to buying a put (and selling bonds) portfolio insurance may be created synthetically. Assume that discount rates are constant and that the value of the portfolio follows a binomial random walk, and denote the

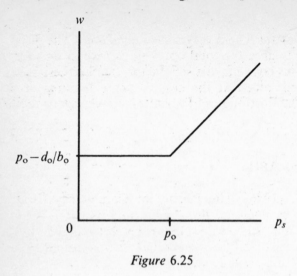

Figure 6.25

put hedge ratio on date t by h_t. Then between dates t and $t+1$ buying a put is equivalent to selling h_t securities and using the proceeds to buy bonds. Thus synthetic insurance may be created by on each date t adjusting the total portfolio so that the proportion h_t of its value is held in bonds and the remainder in the original portfolio.

A problem with this approach is that the assumption that the value of the portfolio follows a binomial random walk is inconsistent with the (more natural) assumption that the prices of the constituent securities follow binomial random walks. For example, assume that the portfolio consists of two securities of equal value and that the price of each follows a binomial random walk with upward and downward moves of α and β. Then the possible portfolio moves are

$$(\alpha, (\alpha+\beta)/2, \beta),$$

which is inconsistent with a binomial random walk. However, despite this theoretical problem the assumption that the value of the portfolio follows a binomial random walk may be a reasonable approximation in practice.

The advantage of synthetic insurance is that puts on the specific portfolio held may not be available. The disadvantage is that, since the total portfolio is revised on each date, transactions costs may be significant, though these costs may be reduced, albeit at the cost of some tracking error, by revising the portfolio only when a large change is required.

BIBLIOGRAPHY

Black, F. (1976) 'The Pricing of Commodity Contracts', *Journal of Financial Economics*, no 3, pp. 167–79.

Black, F. and Scholes, M, (1973) 'The Pricing of Options and Corporate Liabilities', *Journal of Political Economy*, no 81, pp. 637–54.

Chiras, D. P. and Manaster, S. (1978) 'The Information Content of Option Prices and a Test of Market Efficiency', *Journal of Financial Economics*, no 6, pp. 213–34.

Cox, J. C. and Ross, S. A. (1976) 'The Valuation of Options for Alternative Stochastic Processes', *Journal of Financial Economics*, no 3, pp. 145–66.

Cox, J. C., Ross, S. A. and Rubinstein, M. (1979) 'Option Pricing: A Simplified Approach', *Journal of Financial Economics*, no 7, pp. 229–63.

Galai, D. (1978) 'Empirical Tests of Boundary Conditions for CBOE Options', *Journal of Financial Economics*, no 6, pp. 187–211.

Galai, D. (1983) 'A Survey of Empirical Tests of Option Pricing Models' in M. Brenner (ed.) *Option Pricing* (Lexington: Heath).

Ingersoll, J. E. (1989) 'Option Pricing Theory' in J. Eatwell, M. Milgate and P. Newman (eds) *The New Palgrave: Finance* (London: Macmillan).

Merton, R. C. (1973) 'Theory of Rational Option Pricing', *Bell Journal of Economics and Management Science*, no 4, pp. 141–83.

Merton, R. C. (1989) 'Options' in J. Eatwell, M. Milgate and P. Newman (eds) *The New Palgrave: Finance* (London: Macmillan).

Morrison, D. (1967) *Multivariate Statistical Methods* (New York: McGraw-Hill).

Phillips, S. M. and Smith, C. W. (1978) 'Trading Costs for Listed Options: The Implications for Market Efficiency', *Journal of Financial Economics*, no 8, pp. 179–201.

Smith, C. R. (1976) 'Option Pricing: A Review', *Journal of Financial Economics*, no 3, pp. 3–51.

7 Information Arbitrage: Market Efficiency

This chapter explores, by way of a brief coda, one much-discussed implication of the concept of arbitrage: the hypothesis that security prices reflect all available information.

THE EFFICIENT MARKET HYPOTHESIS

We again consider a limited liability security whose payoff occurs on date s only, and whose (positive) price on date t is denoted by p_t. Applying the martingale property on date t gives

$$p_t = \delta_t \hat{E}_t p_{t+1}$$

where δ_t is the single-period discount factor and $\hat{E}_t$ the martingale expectations operator on date t, that is, the conditional martingale expectations operator given the set of states which are possible on that date.

Given some arbitrary probabilities we may write this relation as

$$p_t = \lambda_t E_t p_{t+1}$$

where E_t is the expectation operator under these arbitrary probabilities on date t and

$$\lambda_t = \delta_t \hat{E}_t p_{t+1} / E_t p_{t+1} > 0$$

is a risk-adjusted discount factor on date t, that is, the product of the pure discount factor δ_t and a risk premium

$$\hat{E}_t p_{t+1} / E_t p_{t+1}.$$

The relation

$$\lambda_t E_t p_{t+1} = p_t$$

is known as the (weak form of the) efficient market hypothesis.

The single-period return of the security on date t is

$$r_t = p_{t+1}/p_t - 1.$$

Since p_t is known on date t the expected return on date t is thus

$$E_t r_t = (E_t p_{t+1})/p_t - 1,$$

so that the efficient market hypothesis may also be written as

$$E_t r_t = 1/\lambda_t - 1.$$

The efficient market hypothesis only has empirical content if the risk-adjusted discount factors λ_t are restricted in some way. The simplest (non-trivial) such restriction is that these are constant, that is, that

$$\lambda_t = \lambda,$$

say, on each date t. Under this assumption the (unconditional) covariance between successive returns is

$$\text{cov}(r_t, r_{t+1}) = E_0(r_t - E_0 r_t)(r_{t+1} - E_0 r_{t+1})$$

$$= E_0(r_t - E_0 r_t) r_{t+1} = E_0(E_t(r_t - E_0 r_t) r_{t+1})$$

$$= E_0((r_t - E_0 r_t) E_t r_{t+1}) = E_0((r_t - E_0 r_t)(1/\lambda - 1)$$

$$= (1/\lambda - 1) E_0(r_t - E_0 r_t) = 0.$$

Thus under the restriction that risk-adjusted discount factors are constant the efficient market hypothesis implies that returns are serially uncorrelated.

EVIDENCE

Fama (1965) estimates the first order serial correlations of daily returns of each of the securities in a market index. The average correlation is only 0.026, and the correlations for 73 per cent of the securities are positive while those for the remaining 27 per cent are negative. These figures suggest the existence of some small, but insignificant, positive serial correlation.

An alternative indication of the extent of any positive serial correlation is provided by the number of runs, that is, of sequences of days all of whose returns are of the same sign. If returns are positively correlated then the number of runs should be less than the number expected under the assumption that returns are uncorrelated. Fama finds that although this is the case the discrepancy is only 3 per cent. Thus again, any serial correlation appears to be insignificant.

Fama's results are supported by numerous other investigations. Granger (1975), for example, surveys the results of nine studies, with time intervals ranging from one day to 16 weeks; none of these find any significant serial correlation.

WEAK AND STRONG EFFICIENCY

Tests of the existence of serial correlation are only equivalent to tests of the weak form of the efficient market hypothesis under the restriction that risk-adjusted rates of return are constant, or at least that changes in these rates are of a second order of magnitude. There are, however, numerous tests of the hypothesis under alternative restrictions: indeed, according to Jensen (1988, p. 26) 'no proposition in any of the sciences is better documented'. The findings of such tests are summarised by Malkiel (1989, pp. 127–9) as follows:

> The weak form of the Efficient Market Hypothesis (EMH) asserts that prices fully reflect the information contained in the historical sequence of prices. Thus, investors cannot

devise an investment strategy to yield abnormal profits on the basis of an analysis of past price patterns (a technique known as technical analysis) . . . The empirical evidence presents strong evidence in favour of the weak form of the efficient market hypothesis. The history of stock price movements does not offer investors any information that permits them to outperform a simple buy-and-hold investment strategy.

Weak form efficiency, which follows directly from the absence of arbitrage, at least when risk-adjusted rates of return are constant, implies that information on past prices cannot be used to generate excess profits (that is, profits in excess of those required to compensate for the risk involved).

Intuitively, the absence of arbitrage also implies that no other (publicly) available information can be used to generate excess profits. This hypothesis is known as the semi-strong form of the efficient market hypothesis (as distinct from the strong form, which concerns private information and the possibility of profiting from 'insider trading'). The findings of the numerous tests of semi-strong efficiency are summarised by Malkiel (1989, pp. 127–30) as follows.

The semi-strong form of the EMH asserts that stock prices reflect not only historical price information but also all publicly available information relevant to a company's securities. If markets are efficient in this sense, then an analysis of . . . public information about a company (the technique of fundamental analysis) will not yield abnormal economic profits . . . The empirical evidence suggests that public information is so rapidly impounded into current market prices that fundamental analysis is not likely to be fruitful.

On the efficient market hypothesis in general (including its strong form) Malkiel (1989, p. 131) concludes that 'the empirical evidence in favour of EMH is extremely strong. Probably no other hypothesis in either economics or finance has been more extensively tested'.

Thus intuition accords with reality: neither 'technical' nor 'fundamental' analysis can generate excess profits. But this is not a novel idea: it has been understood at least since Bachelier's seminal work of 1900.

BIBLIOGRAPHY

Bachelier, L. (1900) 'Théorie de la Speculation', *Annales de l'Ecole Normale Supérieure*, no 17, pp. 21–86. Translated by A. J. Boness as 'Theory of Speculation', in P. H. Cootner (ed.) *The Random Character of Stock Market Prices* (Cambridge, Massachusetts: MIT Press, 1967).

Fama, E. (1965) 'The Behavior of Stock Market Prices', *Journal of Business*, no 38, pp. 34–105.

Fama, E. (1970) 'Efficient Capital Markets: A Review of Theory and Empirical Work', *Journal of Business*, no 25, pp. 383–417.

Granger, C. W. J. (1975) 'A Survey of Empirical Studies of Capital Markets', in E. J. Elton and M. J. Gruber (eds) *International Capital Markets* (Amsterdam: North Holland).

Jensen, M. (1988) 'Takeovers: Their Causes and Consequences', *Journal of Economic Perspectives*, no 2(1), pp. 21–48.

Malkiel, B. G. (1989) 'Efficient Market Hypothesis', in J. Eatwell, M. Milgate and P. Newman (eds) *The New Palgrave: Finance* (London: Macmillan).

Index